RISE AND SHINE

A Practical Guide for the Beginning SCIENCE TEACHER

RISE AND SHINE

A Practical Guide for the Beginning SCIENCE TEACHER

Linda Froschauer and Mary L. Bigelow

NSTApress

National Science Teachers Association

Arlington, Virginia

National Science Teachers Association

Claire Reinburg, Director
Jennifer Horak, Managing Editor
Andrew Cooke, Senior Editor
Wendy Rubin, Associate Editor
Agnes Bannigan, Associate Editor
Amy America, Book Acquisitions Coordinator

ART AND DESIGN
Will Thomas Jr., Director
Lucio Bracamontes, Graphic Designer, cover and interior design

PRINTING AND PRODUCTION
Catherine Lorrain, Director

NATIONAL SCIENCE TEACHERS ASSOCIATION
Francis Q. Eberle, PhD, Executive Director
David Beacom, Publisher

1840 Wilson Blvd., Arlington, VA 22201
www.nsta.org/store
For customer service inquiries, please call 800-277-5300.

NSTA is committed to publishing material that promotes the best in inquiry-based science education. However, conditions of actual use may vary, and the safety procedures and practices described in this book are intended to serve only as a guide. Additional precautionary measures may be required. NSTA and the authors do not warrant or represent that the procedures and practices in this book meet any safety code or standard of federal, state, or local regulations. NSTA and the authors disclaim any liability for personal injury or damage to property arising out of or relating to the use of this book, including any of the recommendations, instructions, or materials contained therein.

LIBRARY OF CONGRESS CATALOGING-IN-PUBLICATION DATA
Froschauer, Linda.
  Rise and shine : a practical guide for the beginning science teacher / by Linda Froschauer, Mary L. Bigelow.
    p. cm.
  Includes bibliographical references and index.
  ISBN 978-1-936137-29-9
  1. Science--Study and teaching. 2. Science teachers. 3. First year teachers. I. Bigelow, Mary L., 1949- II. Title.
  Q181.F837 2012
  507.1--dc23
                        2012012217

eISBN 978-1-936959-80-8

FSC
www.fsc.org
MIX
Paper from
responsible sources
FSC® C011935

CONTENTS

INTRODUCTION

THINK BACK TO your first day of school in kindergarten or first grade and how nervous (and excited) you were. That's how nervous (and excited) you'll be on your first day as a science teacher! Even veteran teachers get a few butterflies on the first day when the door opens and the students come into the classroom or lab for the first time.

When you were student teaching or doing your practicum, you walked into a situation that was already set up for you. The classroom or lab was organized, the supplies were inventoried and stored, the safety routines were in place, and the students were accustomed to your cooperating teacher's style. But now you're on your own. It may sound like a paradox, but even though teachers are in a building full of people, teaching can be a lonely profession. It doesn't have to be, but new teachers may feel overwhelmed and hesitant to ask for suggestions or support.

We don't want you to leave this wonderful profession due to a lack of support. Statistics show that half of those who enter teaching leave within the first five years. That is simply unacceptable. We need high-quality teachers to support student learning. We know that the longer you stay in the profession, the more you'll add to and refine your teaching skills. This book was created to address the needs of teachers who are entering the science teaching profession. This includes those who have recently completed their undergraduate studies as well as those who are assigned to teaching a different subject or grade level for the first time. This book can also be helpful to those who are supporting new teachers as mentors or administrators.

We invite you to join us at Community School (CS), a K–12 consolidated school. The heartbeat of CS is in the teachers' lounge. This is where people gather in the morning to grab a cup of coffee and check their mailboxes. It is also where the staff gathers for short breaks, planning periods, and lunch. There always seems to be food available for anyone who wants a quick snack as well as the company of others who are interested in sharing a conversation. Everyone in the building joins in the varied conversations that take place at some point during the day. CS is a large school with many seasoned teachers, as well as several who are new to the school.

As you read the book, you will meet several of the administrators and other science teachers as they provide suggestions and personal comments. We would like for you to meet our new science teachers:

Alberto has been teaching high school biology for two years but is switching to middle school environmental science—new content and a new grade level. "I'm a little nervous about working with younger students. I think I'll need some additional teaching strategies and assessment ideas, but I think my sense of humor will help."

Heather has been a substitute teacher for a year and was recently hired as a full-time elementary science specialist. She will meet with all of the fourth and fifth graders. "This sounds like a dream job! But I'm wondering about how to manage working with all of these students and two different grade levels in the same lab—and the paperwork."

Jason is a recent college graduate in his first teaching assignment, splitting his day between middle school physical science and high school physics classes. "I'm fine with the content, but with two different subjects and grade levels, I think I might get even crazier than I already am. I'd appreciate any ideas to help me get organized. Safety is also a big concern of mine."

Sherrie worked as an industrial chemist for 15 years and is changing careers to be a high school chemistry teacher. "I'm really excited about sharing my real-world science experiences. I can manage a lab, but I need some suggestions on classroom management. I also need suggestions on getting to know 100-plus students and communicating with parents."

Tanya is a recent college graduate beginning her first year as a high school Earth science teacher. "I did not have a lab when I did my student teaching, but at CS I do. (Yay!) I'll need advice on setting up and maintaining a lab and inventories. Like Jason, I worry about safety. I have lots of questions. I hope that I can find other teachers to help me."

The *NSTA Reports* column "Ms. Mentor" has been the inspiration for including Ms. Mentor as a contributor to the discussions. Ms. Mentor is a highly respected retired science teacher who volunteers to work with new teachers. The new teachers at CS have been urged to use her as a resource, and she'll respond to their questions with insights and suggestions at the beginning of each chapter.

Enter the teachers' lounge using the first three chapters of *Rise and Shine: A Practical Guide for the Beginning Science Teacher*. These chapters include suggestions for starting the first few weeks of school. The rest of the book covers safety, organization, teaching and assessment strategies, and professional development. A comprehensive discussion of these topics would take several volumes, but this book is designed to be an overview for the new teacher. Read through to the end or select chapters that meet your immediate needs and save the rest for later. We designed the book to provide you with the opportunity to start reading wherever it makes the most sense for you. We encourage you to discuss the ideas, suggestions, and strategies with a partner (in your school or through an online community) or share your insights with your mentor.

We have provided many lists of suggestions in the text. Some are ideas from which you can pick and choose, indicated by a bullet (•). Others are checklists of steps to follow as you proceed through a specific strategy, as shown by a check-off box (❏). You will also find frequent references to other sections of the book, as well as to additional resources at the end of each chapter and online appendixes, identified by the arrow (→). The resources can help you begin gathering the materials for your own professional library. We have provided most of the appendix documents in a word-processing format to allow you to personalize the materials. The online appendixes and internet resources can be accessed online at *www.nsta.org/riseandshine*. The resources will be updated periodically to reflect newly available resources.

Although we wrote the book for you as you enter your new science position, we hope you will find the information valuable throughout your career, which we hope is long and successful. We both have had moments when we looked at our students as they were enthusiastically engaged in investigations and we thought, "It doesn't get any better than this!"

Best wishes for great success and fulfillment,
Linda and Mary

CHAPTER 1
OFF TO A GOOD START

Dear Ms. Mentor,

What skills should students develop to become lifelong learners in science?

Heather

Dear Heather,

In science department meetings, teachers often agonize over what and how much content to cover. We lament that students don't seem to remember much content from one year to the next. Demonstrating and performing inquiry and in-depth study often take a backseat to presenting content that will be on a final exam or state test.

But when referring to skills, one of my favorite quotations is often attributed to Einstein: "Education is what's left after you've forgotten everything." In other words, even though we might not remember everything (content), we should be able to apply our experiences (skills) to new situations.

A principal once asked about my philosophy of learning. I had never written any formal document, so I listed the "big picture" skills I wanted students to take away from my courses:

- *Problem solving and inquiry*: Beyond simply following directions, students should learn how to work through new situations by asking questions, discussing, doing active listening, defining problems, designing investigations, observing, finding and evaluating information, and communicating (both verbally and graphically).
- *Risk taking*: Students should have opportunities and support to get out of their intellectual comfort zones to investigations where "correct" answers may not be known ahead of time, if at all.
- *Imagination and creativity*: When given opportunities and encouragement, students often surprise and delight us with how they use their talents and interests.

- *Dedication*: It's easy to be distracted, but seeing a task through to completion, building on one's strengths, working on one's weaknesses, and striving for more than mediocrity are real boosts to self-esteem—even better than a teacher saying "good job."
- *Enthusiasm and enjoyment*: Learning is intrinsically interesting and part of what makes us human. Not all learning experiences have to be fun, but good teachers can make any topic interesting with passion and by providing students with engaging classroom activities.

These "skills" are not measureable with standardized tests, and they evolve as students are exposed to science content and learn subject-specific procedures. The skills require modeling by the teacher: If a teacher is not a risk-taker or has little enthusiasm for a topic, it's hard for students to develop that attribute. It's important to make the classroom a "safe" place where students can practice with and apply these skills to a variety of situations. Teachers should recognize and support student efforts in these areas and help students see the connections among science topics and other content areas and within their own lives.

Independent learning beyond the classroom is based on skills such as the ones listed above. Not all students will pursue a science-related career or have the same passion for the subject as their teachers. But they will be voters, taxpayers, parents, employees, business owners, travelers, professionals, and hobbyists who will need not only basic content knowledge but also the skills to be lifelong learners in science-related issues. How many of our schools' mission statements address this need? What are we doing to make sure our students are prepared for the future?

—Ms. Mentor

_____

As you begin your science teaching career, you will have many questions. The best place to start is to ask questions of yourself. You may not be able to answer all of the questions quickly or casually, but they should be food for thought. Spend time thinking about each question, and take into consideration how the process can benefit you as you create an exceptional learning environment and become the teacher you want to be.

Your Role as a Teacher

As a teacher, you obviously teach students as your main role. That sounds easy enough, especially if you know the subject matter well. But there are many issues that can get in the way, and being aware of these issues is the first step to becoming an excellent teacher from whom students can learn. This book will provide you with information concerning many of the topics you should consider as you plan and implement instruction.

Professional educators have core beliefs and understandings that help guide them and provide a focus. Boards of education frequently establish a set of core beliefs. The following beliefs appear on many lists (the list below was adapted from Children's Defense Fund 2011; Durham Public Schools 2008; New Leaders for New Schools 2011; and Redmond School District 2007):

- All children can learn.
- Children learn in different ways and at different rates.
- Effective teachers exhibit positive attitudes toward all students at all times.
- Expectations should be set high. Most students will reach only as high as you expect them to reach.
- Success builds on itself—one success brings about other successes.
- Effective teachers know how to design lessons for student mastery.
- Teachers are role models at all times.
- Teachers are in control of what happens in the classroom.
- Teachers can make a difference in a child.
- Not every lesson will be a resounding success, but every lesson will provide insight to what should be done in the future.
- Safety in the science classroom is paramount.

> Now is the time to seriously consider your role as a teacher. Don't try to establish this later in the year when you are harried and time is limited. You'll want to revisit this statement later to review what you have written, but if you have considered it thoroughly, you'll probably find it will serve you well for a very long time.
>
> —Pat, grade 11 science teacher

Your Role as a Team Member

Teaching is a profession that provides a support system. When you are hired into a school, you have an automatic connection to all of the teachers in that building. However, you do not have an automatic right to their help and support. Few teachers will find others in the building knocking on the door, asking if they require help. If you find yourself in the position of receiving this kind of support, take advantage of it and be appreciative of anything others may provide to help you. Most new teachers must seek out and ask for support. Many have said that teaching is an isolated profession, but it doesn't have to be if you keep your door open (both literally and figuratively). Be open, invite others into your classroom, and become an active member of your teaching community. (→ See Chapter 6, "Your Attitude Matters," and Chapter 11, "Finding Support.")

> The interview process and questions will be a good indicator of what the school system is like and what expectations you will be required to fulfill.
>
> —Ty, middle school principal

Your Role in the Learning Community

You have been hired for one purpose—to help students learn and achieve. Teaching has nothing to do with what the teacher covers; it has everything to do with what students learn. Therefore, it is important that you create learning opportunities, not just teaching opportunities. You will find many suggestions for how this is accomplished throughout this book and in other sources. You can also tap into your undergraduate experience for information concerning learning progressions, research, and lesson plans.

As an employee of the school system, you must follow regulations and fulfill expectations in addition to those involving student learning. Some of these are school or district regulations, while others are state laws:

- Learn the rules and policies of the school and district.
- Honor school rules, even if you disagree with them.
- Do not ever leave your students unsupervised.
- Maintain a safe environment, and be especially diligent in the lab.
- Report serious student problems, such as substance abuse.
- Report child abuse.
- Don't allow bullying, harassment, or rough play.
- Be cautious in the way you touch children.
- Don't allow a student to leave school with anyone who is not authorized to take the child.
- Know the laws of privacy and confidentiality, and don't break them.
- If students confide in you, don't agree to not tell anyone else what they have said.
- Call in sick only when you are ill.
- Don't give students free time in which they have nothing to do.

I Chose Science Teaching Because ...

Why did you go into the teaching profession? Were you inspired by a teacher you had and admired? Is this a profession in which many in your family have been involved? Dig deep. Consider the basic reason why you are in the classroom. This might be a good time to write down the reason you selected this profession rather than any other career. Once you have written down your reason, put your paper somewhere close at hand, where you can read it often, especially in times of stress or when you're having second thoughts. (By the way, it is guaranteed that you will have second thoughts during your first year on the job.)

Your Teaching Philosophy

Sherrie

I know I should have a philosophy, something I can reflect on that will help me keep my vision for education in mind. But I have no idea how to write one that will serve as a valuable tool for me. Where do I start?

Your teaching philosophy can serve as a touchstone for you as you progress in your career, as well as provide a focal point in your teaching. It will help you maintain a clear vision, verify your teaching decisions, and modify your teaching behaviors. Keep in mind that your philosophy is a work in progress and will change as you learn more about science teaching and your students. Therefore, you should occasionally revisit and modify your philosophy. Think about what role each of these components plays in your overall view of teaching and how you interact with students:

- Sense of fairness
- Ability to be flexible
- Positive attitude
- Consistent approach
- Sense of humor
- High expectations for yourself and your students

Your philosophy of teaching should specifically reflect your personal values and the needs of both your students and your teaching community. You should also consider your teaching position, both the subject matter and age of students, in your statement. There are several components to a philosophy; the following list may provide you with points to consider when you construct yours. Be sure to limit your statement to one or two pages.

❏ The goals: Although you may not state them at the beginning of your philosophy statement, it's important to start with where you want to end—your goals. Identify your goals as a teacher. Be sure these goals are attainable. The rest of your statement is going to support the attainment of these goals, so be sure they are not vague or overstatements that can't be attained. Here are some of the goals you might include:

  ○ Learning or refreshing your understanding of the science content included in your class or course
  ○ Fostering critical thinking
  ○ Attaining lifelong learning skills
  ○ Interacting with manipulatives
  ○ Using technology in investigations
  ○ Developing problem-solving skills
  ○ Infusing a love of science
  ○ Creating an atmosphere for understanding of the scientific enterprise
  ○ Covering additional topics that are currently important in education and endorsed by your educational community

❏ How to get there: When you have a clear sense of your goals and objectives, you can explain methods you use to attain these goals:

  ○ Explain the connection of your goals to learning theory, cognitive development, and curriculum design.
  ○ Explain specific strategies you use to instruct students, such as inquiry. Be sure to tie these strategies directly to your goals.
  ○ If your curriculum is not specifically outlined for you, explain how you make curriculum decisions.
  ○ Include mention of the role that national and state science standards play in your decisions.
  ○ If you have personally developed instructional materials, be sure to include them.

A teacher once told me that he intentionally set out to have at least one new learning experience each year. The topic is unimportant (although it should be of interest). The critical piece is that it would provide a true learning experience, including the feeling of ignorance that comes with new learning. That feeling provided him with different ways of dealing with new experiences, as well as empathy for what students may experience.

—Richard, science department chair

- ○ Consider what you mean by learning and what a successful learning situation looks like.
- ○ Include interactions with students and the importance of those interactions.
- ❑ How you measure effectiveness: Connect your strategies to your goals and explain how you measure the effectiveness of what you do. Both formative and summative assessments should play a role. This should be linked to student learning outcomes rather than how many topics you have covered or how many science lab lessons you have taught in a semester.
- ❑ Why you are teaching science: This is the place to go beyond the textual material and curriculum. Be grand in your explanation of why you teach. Explain the rewards of teaching, why teaching is important to you, how you (as a science teacher) can make the world a better place, the ideals you bring to the profession, and/or how you can make a difference in the lives of your students.
- ❑ How you will continue to grow as a teacher: It's important to include formal and informal professional development and other activities that will help you grow professionally.

There are many examples of teaching philosophies online to serve as inspiration as you prepare yours. (→ See Resources and a sample philosophy in Online Appendix 1.1.)

Conclusion

You may initially think of the topics in this chapter as unimportant or material you have contemplated in the past. But spend some time with each item thinking about your roles and responsibilities. You will find that as the year progresses, you will be caught up in many responsibilities and have little time to reflect on why you teach and how you fit into the overall teaching community. The documents you prepare while reading this chapter will serve as touchstones throughout the year.

Resources *(www.nsta.org/riseandshine)*

Teaching Philosophy

Developing a Philosophy of Teaching Statement: *http://spinner.cofc.edu/~cetl/Essays/ DevelopingaPhilosophyofTeaching.html?referrer=webcluster&*
Getting Started on Your Teaching Philosophy: *www1.umn.edu/ohr/teachlearn/ tutorials/philosophy/start/index.html*
Writing a Teaching Philosophy Statement: *www.celt.iastate.edu/teaching/philosophy.html*
Writing Your Own Educational Philosophy: *www.edulink.org/portfolio/philosophies.htm*

Online Appendix

1.1. Sample Philosophy

CHAPTER 2
BEFORE YOU OPEN THE CLASSROOM OR LAB DOOR FOR STUDENTS

Tanya

Dear Ms. Mentor,

I'm excited about my new teaching job but a little nervous. How should I get ready for the first day of school?

Dear Tanya,

There are many sources of advice for new teachers, but we science teachers have additional responsibilities: planning hands-on activities, managing a laboratory, maintaining inventories, adhering to safety requirements, and staying current with the content.

Ask your supervisor for a copy of your school's science curriculum and copies of the textbook and teacher guide. Familiarize yourself with the content topics, big ideas, essential questions, learning goals, activities, and assessments. Highlight the equipment and materials you'll need for the first unit so you can make sure you have what you need to get started.

Take some time to organize and arrange your classroom or lab. Find out what basic safety equipment is available since that will affect what kind of activities you can plan. Ask other staff members ahead of time if notebooks and other consumable materials have been ordered and what technology will be available for classroom use.

As you tour your new school or attend meetings and workshops, introduce yourself to other teachers and support staff. Don't worry if you forget their names—you'll learn them soon enough! Contact the technology coordinator or librarian to obtain passwords for online resources for which the district has memberships or licenses.

Use the district website to learn about your school and the other schools in the district. Look at the current calendar to get a sense of when events such as open houses, end of marking periods, and holiday breaks occur. Check out the student and faculty handbooks to learn about the procedures you'll need to follow. Look at how other teachers have structured their district web pages or blogs. Start to plan what you will put on your own page, including an introduction to your professional background and your interests related to science.

Begin to assemble your professional resources. Some science teachers like to wear a lab coat or apron, and you may want to have your own goggles rather than use the student ones. Find out the dress guidelines for teachers and make sure you have professional, comfortable attire to start the year.

Whether we like it or not, teachers are considered role models and are held to higher standards of decorum and behavior. This would be a good time to purge any social media sites of inappropriate or unprofessional information and photos. Ask for your school e-mail address and begin to use it for professional correspondence. Use a separate account for your personal communications.

Visit the school's community if you're not already familiar with it, both in person and online. Learn about the local history and explore any museums, parks, or nature centers in the region. Note the location of the public library and whether your students have access to it.

If possible, reserve two or three weeks before the first day of school to prepare yourself for the year (and to have a little breathing room). During this time, your district may offer teacher workshops. Take advantage of these to upgrade your skills and meet other teachers.

—Ms. Mentor

Walking into the school the first day is overwhelming. I want to feel comfortable in the environment before the students arrive. Where do I start?

Jason

It's a few weeks before the start of the school year. You walk into the school to pick up the key to your classroom or lab. You're excited and perhaps a little apprehensive, and you get a flashback to your first day of kindergarten. There are many similarities between your first days as a student and your first days as a teacher: meeting new people, getting to know the school building, and learning the procedures.

Meet the People Who Are Important to You in Doing Your Job

If you've been assigned a mentor as part of your school's induction or orientation program, he or she should contact you to set up time to meet and go over the information and procedures you need at the beginning of the school year. If your school does not have a mentor program, ask your principal for the name of another science teacher who can help you get started as an unofficial mentor. (→ See Chapter 11 for more on mentors.)

Assuming you have already met the principal during the interview process and follow-up conversations, the next person to get to know is the principal's secretary. In most schools, this is the go-to person if you have questions about school procedures. Several other people will also be important to you throughout the year:

- ❏ Custodians
- ❏ Your team leader or department chairperson
- ❏ Those who are on your team or teach the same grade level/subject
- ❏ Safety officer (chemical hygiene officer)
- ❏ Librarian
- ❏ Nurse
- ❏ Technology coordinator
- ❏ Person who runs the copy machine
- ❏ Guidance counselor

> Sometimes, being the best teacher you can be means knowing how to enlist the help of others in a variety of situations.
>
> —Shayna, special education teacher

Seek them out before school starts, learn their names, and ask lots of questions. You're probably not the only new teacher in your school. Forming a support group with your fellow novices is a good way to share ideas and experiences and know that you're not alone. You can meet additional resource people through professional Listservs, blogs, online communities, or teacher groups on social media sites.

Know the Curriculum

Don't make assumptions about the curriculum. It's important for you to know what's expected of your students, so you should become familiar with state frameworks or academic standards. However, you'll find the frameworks and standards do not tell you the specific curriculum for your grade level or subject. If a science curriculum document isn't handed to you immediately, ask for it (it may be an online document). Also ask if there is any support material that will help you with your instruction. This should be done as soon as you know you have acquired a specific position in the school system. It's your responsibility to prepare lessons that align with the curriculum.

You may receive a detailed document with a curriculum sequence that specifies the content topics, big ideas, essential questions, learning goals, activities, materials and resources, suggestions for differentiation, extensions or accommodations, and assessments for each unit of instruction in your particular subject or grade level (e.g., high school chemistry, middle school life science, grade 5 general science, elementary school topics). You also may be handed a teacher's edition of the selected textbook and simply told that the book serves as the curriculum. You won't know what lies ahead for you and your preparation of lessons until you receive the documentation provided by your school system.

Know the content of the science you are to teach, as well as the skills you will develop along with the content. Also be aware of where these skills and content are within the learning progression.

If you receive a complete curriculum guide, your first task is to become familiar with it. If it is in an electronic format, you may need some guidance in navigating it at first. Be certain you understand the science content, determine if you have all of the materials and equipment you will need to conduct the first few lessons, and begin organizing your own files and strategies for fulfilling the required study. If the textbook model is followed by your school system, check with a colleague or department chair concerning what has already been done to implement the curriculum. (→ See Chapter 7, "Teaching Strategies.")

Explore Your Environment

As you open the door to your classroom or lab for the first time, be prepared for anything. The room may be in pristine condition, with everything organized, labeled, color-coded, and ready for the students. Or it may take a scavenger hunt to find anything. At the extreme, the room may be totally empty except for the furniture.

Whether the teacher's desk is at the front or back of the room or in an office, note what supplies are there. You'll need a basic supply of paper clips, pencils, index cards, sticky notes, a stapler and staples, folders, and paper. Look for student consumables such as notebooks or folders. Find out from the school's secretary how to request these supplies if you need them. Find out about recycling efforts at your school. You will more than likely want to supplement what the school provides with some of your own items. (→ See Online Appendix 2.1 for a shopping list.)

Be sure you have the keys to the storage room and to the lockable cabinets—and lock them. If your room is not on the main floor, find out if there is an elevator, if there is a key for the elevator, and how to get a key. (→ See Chapter 5, "Safety in the Laboratory.")

Wander around the building while it's quiet and empty. Note the location of the main entrance, the administrative offices, the cafeteria, and student restrooms in relation to your classroom. Find the faculty room, the adult restrooms (keys may be needed), the coffee pot and vending machines, and the copy machine (you may need a code). Peek into the other labs and classrooms for ideas. Check out the library and other areas, such as the computer labs, the guidance office, and the nurse's suite. Some other teachers and staff may be in the building, so introduce yourself.

Take a walk around the outside of the school. Are there any possible locations for outdoor science activities, such as a nature area or even a grassy yard? Look for evidence of science activities such as gardens, bird feeders, or a weather station. Determine if there is a school policy concerning taking students outside during

> Ask your department chair how much leeway you have in following the curriculum. Are you expected to be on the same chapter as other teachers at all times? Can you rearrange the topics? Are there common assessments?
>
> —Dwayne, grade 9 science teacher

> Many teachers keep file cabinets filled with folders containing lesson plans, resources, units, or themes. Our team uses three-ring binders that contain our lesson plans and resources and find this much easier for referencing materials, bringing ideas to team meetings, and sharing.
>
> —Joclyn, grade 7 science teacher

class time. You may need to notify the office, take your cell phone with you, or have another adult help supervise.

Know Your Technology

The amount and kind of technology to use in the science lab varies from school to school or grade level to grade level. Ask the technology coordinator what technology will be available to you in the classroom or lab, such as laptops, tablets, an interactive whiteboard, student response system, probeware, cameras, calculators, document viewers, or projection attachments for microscopes. If this equipment is shared among classrooms, ask the technology coordinator how to schedule a time for use. Find out about the internet connectivity in your classroom or lab and the location of printers available for you to use. Also ask the technology coordinator if students have logins and passwords for accessing the school network and its resources.

If the school does not provide a laptop you can take home, invest in some USB flash drives you can use to take files to work on at home or use an online service to save and access files. Find out what passwords or protocols you need to access the school network from home. Review the acceptable use policy (which you probably signed along with all of the other paperwork) to determine what you can and cannot do with school-owned technology.

How does the technology fit into the classroom? If each student uses a laptop, is the student's desk big enough to accommodate it along with other materials? If laptops are stored in a cart, can the cart be placed near an outlet to recharge the computers? How many teachers share the laptops? Are there enough outlets at the lab stations for microscopes and other electronic equipment?

Do you need assistance connecting with and using the interactive board or with other projection devices? Ask about workshops or tutorials on the district's student management system that is used for attendance and grading. If you must submit attendance lists, lesson plans, grades, other reports, and curriculum updates electronically, ask how to become familiar with the system. Ask if you are required to have a web page and if there is a standard format for teacher web pages.

Read Your Teacher Handbook

The devil is in the details, and there are many details involved in your daily teaching life. Many of these will become second nature—topics you won't even think about as you become acclimated to your new career. Therefore, it's quite possible that people will forget to give you detailed information about how to function within the parameters of the building rules and expectations.

The following information should be available to you in a teacher or faculty handbook. If you don't receive a handbook, ask for it. If it lacks some of these components, seek out the answers:

> I didn't have a lockable location in my room that could contain sensitive documents like my personal student records and notes. I found a drawer that would accommodate a padlock and use that for these materials.
>
> —Pat, grade 11 science teacher

> We have professional development opportunities that include strategies for using the new equipment in the school, such as our interactive whiteboards. These sessions are held after school and teams of teachers attend together, providing them with an opportunity to share information and support one another as they use the equipment.
>
> —Richard, science department chair

Schedules

- ☐ School calendar
- ☐ Bell schedules
- ☐ Meeting schedules—team, grade level, department, faculty, professional development
- ☐ Student grading periods, test dates, and deadlines

Faculty Attendance

- ☐ Notifying the office of your absence
- ☐ Acquiring a substitute
- ☐ Creating substitute plans

Teacher Duties and Responsibilities

- ☐ Homeroom
- ☐ Hall duty
- ☐ Recess and lunch duty
- ☐ Study halls
- ☐ Dismissal and bus duty
- ☐ Extracurricular activities

Student Attendance

- ☐ Attendance taking and reporting
- ☐ Late passes and tardies
- ☐ Written excuses
- ☐ Excused vs. unexcused absences and tardies
- ☐ Preparation of student work in advance of an absence
- ☐ Pull-out programs

Homework

- ☐ Makeup work
- ☐ School guidelines concerning homework

Grading

- ☐ Grading system (e.g., online system, grade books, maintaining records)
- ☐ Report cards (If a sample is not provided, ask to see one.)
- ☐ Progress reports
- ☐ Parent conferences
- ☐ Extracurricular eligibility
- ☐ Family Educational Rights and Privacy Act (FERPA) confidentiality

Behavior Rules

- ☐ Hallways
- ☐ Classroom
- ☐ Arrival and dismissal
- ☐ Dress code or guidelines

❏ Lockers
❏ Procedures for reporting infractions

Student Safety

❏ Fire drills, severe weather drills
❏ Evacuations
❏ Lockdowns
❏ Acceptable Use Policy (AUP) for student access to technology
❏ Emergency school closing (notifications, responsibilities)

Special Events

❏ Field trips
❏ Assemblies
❏ Guest speakers

As a science teacher, you will also need to know about guidelines and routines that might not be in the teacher's handbook. (→ See Chapter 5, "Safety in the Laboratory.")

❏ Food in the science classroom (in a word—don't)
❏ Science department guidelines
❏ Animals in the classroom
❏ Reporting of safety issues
❏ School policies concerning lab safety

> I have made my teacher's handbook a personal reference. I've placed it in a three-ring binder and added information that is important to me. This is also where I keep phone numbers, e-mail addresses, and other information that I need in a handy place.
>
> —Dale, grade 3 teacher

Study Your Schedule and Class List

At the secondary level or in departmentalized situations, you'll need to be very organized if you teach more than one subject. If a homeroom class meets in your lab, remember to keep all lab equipment out of reach for those few minutes. Get into the habit of locking the lab and storage area when you're not in the room. Check to see how many students you have in each class. Having classes with more than 24 students (NSTA 2007) will limit the number and kinds of lab activities you can safely do. (→ See Resources for NSTA's position statement and Chapter 5, "Safety in the Laboratory.")

Veteran teachers want their class lists as soon as they can get them. They look over the list to help them determine seating arrangements, identify students in their classes who may have special needs, determine initial cooperative learning groups, and begin the process of learning student names. If you receive a list and it doesn't have any indication of special needs that students may have, see your administrator or team leader immediately. Find out who can provide you with information concerning those students who may be in special classes, who have medical needs, and who have an individualized learning plan. If you can determine who taught these students during the prior school year, you will also have an advantage. This person can provide you with a wealth of knowledge that will not be found in student files.

I will see more than 100 students each day for my science class. How can I quickly get to know my students?

Heather

One of the most valuable tools you can access is a school yearbook from the prior school year (the library probably has one). It will provide you with photos of students as well as a glimpse into the culture of the school. Can you imagine how impressed students would be if you know their names as soon as they walk in the door? It makes them feel important to you as individuals and lets them know you do know who they are and can follow up on their behavior. It will be impossible to learn a lot of names before the first day of school, but you can do simple things such as displaying the school mascot or wearing school colors to let students know that you are aware of the school's culture. (→ See Chapter 3 for more on getting to know your students.)

Examine Your Inventory of Materials and Equipment

Having an inventory will provide you with the information you will use repeatedly as you plan lessons. Some of your lessons may be generated based on what you have available, while others will require that you find the materials and equipment necessary to conduct the activity. It's important to determine what you have on hand, but don't feel that you have to do a complete inventory at this time. (→ See Chapter 5 for more on lab equipment and supplies.)

Check with your department chair or principal to determine when the budget is established. You may be asked about your needs for the next school term as early as December. If that is the case, you will want to deal with creating or updating a more extensive inventory within the next few weeks. If you annotate your lesson plans throughout the year, you'll have a running list of items you want and need, including consumables to be replaced each year.

In some elementary and middle schools, there is a central science area where equipment, supplies, and kits are stored. Ask your principal or department chairperson how to access these materials and spend some time browsing through what is available. If there is no central area, find out who is the go-to person for materials such as microscopes, magnifiers, magnets, flower pots, metersticks, goggles, balances, or thermometers. It is important to find and explore these materials before you begin planning lessons.

At the secondary level, there probably are storage rooms. These are often connected to the laboratories (and should be locked at all times). Browse through what you have access to in your lab, and ask the department chair to give you a tour of the other labs and storage areas to get a sense of what is in the school science inventory.

I take pictures of my classes during the first few days. The pictures help me learn the names of students by comparing the class list to the photos each morning. I then post these photos on a bulletin at the end of the school year. Students enjoy seeing how they have changed during the year.

—Sharon, grade 5 teacher

Make "Safety First" Your Motto

How can I be certain that I have everything in my classroom needed for safety precautions and that they are in proper working order?

Tanya

Begin by looking at the safety guidelines developed by your board of education. Many of the guidelines will deal with safety in common areas such as hallways, the lunchroom, and school buses. In some cases, they may also address the safety requirements of classrooms in which science lessons take place.

Many secondary schools have a formal document that students (and perhaps parents) sign to indicate they are aware of laboratory safety. If your science department does not have one, consider using Safety in the Science Classroom from NSTA (→ see Resources).

Determine if you are allowed to leave your classroom or the building with your students to conduct science lessons. Also identify necessary paperwork, permissions, and safety guidelines needed for all field trips, including those close to school. (→ See Chapter 7 for more on field trips.)

Contact your safety officer. Ask this person to check your room to be sure all of the equipment is in safe working order. Determine what safety devices are required or recommended by the state department of education. Read the safety guidelines for your state. In most states, these guidelines can be found at the department of education's website. These will cover the types of equipment and materials that should be available to you, as well as restrictions on the use of many materials and live animals.

At a minimum, at the elementary level you should have a fire extinguisher, fire blanket, goggles, and goggle sanitizer in your classroom. At the secondary level, your lab should have these as well as an eyewash station, a safety shower, master turnoff valves for water and gas, and adequate ventilation (including fume hoods). NSTA has publications on safety for elementary, middle, and high schools. (→ See Chapter 5, "Safety in the Laboratory.")

Create a Positive and Inviting Classroom Environment for Learning

As a beginning teacher, I don't have many teaching materials to exhibit in my classroom. What can I do to make my classroom look inviting?

Jason

Your classroom or lab should look like you are ready to begin teaching and learning from the very first day. Don't leave boxes of materials that require your attention

> If you have a chemical cabinet or closet, be sure you know how each of the chemicals should be stored. I walked into a chemistry room and found the teacher had arranged all of the bottles alphabetically. We worked together with the safety officer to store them correctly.
>
> —Richard, science department chair

stacked around the room. Even if you need to stack some things in the closet for the first few days until you can get to them, make the room look organized and ready for learning.

Prepare bulletin boards, bookshelves, and equipment for immediate use. Provide engaging exhibits and display boards that will appeal to the students in your class. An easy way to begin is to exhibit science equipment with labels to identify their purpose. Create a bulletin board that covers some of the topics you will study in science during the year. Word walls, safety guidelines, and current events can be used on bulletin boards too. Some other "science-y" things to attract student interest could include house plants, an aquarium, a collection of objects (e.g., shells, simple machines), or artifacts related to your first unit of study.

Set up areas of the room where students will always be able to find the type of information and materials they need for investigations. A section of your bulletin board should be reserved for the big idea or theme of the unit, assignments, and a daily or weekly class schedule of topics and events. Use a separate board for emergency procedures and important notices. Reserve a table or shelf for trays with lab materials for student access. Provide baskets or trays that contain pencils, markers, rulers, and scrap paper. Have a set place for students to keep their science notebooks and turn in assignments. (→ See Chapter 4 for more on classroom organization.)

Hang up framed copies of your diplomas, teaching certificate, and any awards or recognitions you've received. Put out a few artifacts to introduce yourself to the students. But avoid turning the classroom into a museum dedicated to your favorite sports teams or personal interests.

Your classroom should look like all students can be successful in your science class and will enjoy being successful. The room should convey joy and reflect student interests and accomplishments. Let your enthusiasm show.

> It's important to let students know if there are materials or things in the room that are off-limits—my desk is one of those places. Students may not touch things on my desk, but they have access to anything else that is not under lock and key.
>
> —Dale, grade 3 teacher

Consider the Classroom or Lab Arrangement

Don't underestimate the power of arranging (and rearranging) your classroom or lab environment for optimal learning. Arrange your tables or desks to facilitate communication. Think about what you will ask students to do in this room. Will they work alone, with a partner, or as a team? They will probably work in many configurations. You may need to move desks and tables to accomplish all of the varied activities, but a setting you will frequently use should begin your year.

Think about what your room or lab will look like when it's inhabited by a class of students. Visualize how you'll rearrange the room for the following activities:

- Large-group activities, such as a review, giving directions, or a discussion: Typically, desks or tables are arranged in single or double rows, but many teachers prefer an open U arrangement, if space permits, to get all students involved.
- Individual work, such as assessments or writing activities
- Partners and small groups: Can students push their desks or tables together?

- Student access to materials and equipment they will use
- Flat surfaces for conducting investigations
- Labs or learning stations, especially if the room does not have separate lab tables or benches
- Storage of long-term or ongoing projects

As you think of various arrangements, be sure that all students can see the board, projection screen, or interactive whiteboard. Can they get to the sinks and equipment centers? Can you and the students move around freely without tripping over cords or backpacks? Are your room arrangements appropriate for students with disabilities? How will you modify the room for students who use adaptive or assistive technologies such as microphones, auditory devices, document viewers, or service dogs? Finally, consider safety. Be sure to provide ample pathways for exiting the room in case of an emergency or moving away from hazards that may occur. (→ See Chapter 4 for more on classroom management.)

> I move my tables around to meet the needs of working with a partner or with various team sizes. To assist us in easily moving the tables and avoid scraping the floors, I placed floor protectors on each of the table legs.
>
> —Joclyn, grade 7 science teacher

Be Prepared

No one is going to tell you what to do during the most critical day of school—the first day. You are responsible for creating the atmosphere and tone that your classroom will provide for the entire year and beyond. The expectations, routines, and procedures that you put in place will help you and your students maintain an atmosphere that is both enjoyable and conducive to learning. Don't underestimate the power of that first day. Once the tone is set, it may be difficult to change it. (→ See Chapter 4, "Creating an Environment for Learning.")

Conclusion

After reading Chapters 1 and 2, you should have a fairly comfortable feeling for what is to come next—preparations for facing your class for the first time. The next chapter will help you set the tone and prepare for your first critical week of school.

Resources *(www.nsta.org/riseandshine)*

NSTA Resources

NSTA position statement: Liability of science educators for laboratory safety. *www.nsta.org/about/positions/liability.aspx*

Safety in the Science Classroom: *www.nsta.org/pdfs/SafetyInTheScienceClassroom.pdf*

Online Appendix

2.1 New Teacher's Shopping List

CHAPTER 3
THE FIRST WEEK OF SCHOOL

> **Jason**
>
> Dear Ms. Mentor,
>
> I'm teaching two different subjects (high school physics and middle school physical science). How can I organize and manage my lesson plans and other resources?

Dear Jason,

Creating a system for lesson planning is time-consuming at first (even for one subject), and you'll modify it as you discover what works best for you. It's worth the effort—at the end of the year, you'll have a complete record for the next time you teach the courses. It's much more efficient to revise and adapt rather than re-create the lessons.

My colleagues used to call me the binder queen of planning (I've since progressed to electronic files). Rather than storing the intact curriculum document on the shelf, I took it apart and put the unit plans in a binder (a separate binder for each course). I then inserted my lesson plans and other documents for each unit.

For lesson plans, the best thing I ever did was get rid of the spiral "Plan Book" with its 2 × 3 in. block for each class period. There wasn't enough room to record the plan for an entire lesson other than a cryptic "pp. 52–56, #1–5" or "Algae Lab," which was not much help the following year.

Find out if your school has a lesson plan template. If you're using a framework such as Understanding by Design or the BSCS 5E Instructional Model, there may be lesson templates posted on the project website. If you don't have a suggested template, create one for yourself electronically. Here are some features to include (noting that a lesson may span several class periods):

- Lesson title and dates
- Unit goals (or themes, essential questions, big ideas, standards) supported by the lesson
- Lesson objectives or goals
- Description of the lesson's content topics and key vocabulary
- Introduction to activate prior knowledge (e.g., warm-up activity, recap of previous class period, an interesting anecdote or story)
- Instructional activities (discussions, lab investigations, cooperative learning activities, informal assessments, opportunities for practice or application, readings, multimedia use, homework)
- Lesson assessments and rubrics (quiz, summary, group presentation, lab report, checklists, notebook entry, observation) correlated to the objectives
- Materials needed (web resources, supplemental texts, technology, handouts, lab materials, notebooks, office supplies)
- Adaptations for students with special needs or extensions for students beyond the basic objectives

During the lesson, annotate the plan, reflecting on what went well and what did not work (and what you did to fix it). Describe any modifications you made to activities or assessments.

Use the organizational features on your computer (and save backups on a flash drive, the school server, or an online file-sharing site). Have a color-coded folder for each course and subfolders for each unit and lesson. Archive your presentations, photos, podcasts, and video clips, as well as copies of lesson plans, handouts, and assessments.

In addition to electronic files, I still like the concept of binders where I can flip through an entire unit without opening lots of files. Once a binder queen, always a binder queen!

—Ms. Mentor

THE WAY YOU begin the school year will affect everything that occurs in your classroom and with your colleagues for the remainder of the year—and beyond. When you were student teaching, your cooperating teacher had already set the stage for you. But now starting the school year is your responsibility. Therefore, it is important to dedicate time and energy to this important start.

First Day Fears

It's normal to feel nervous about the first day of school. Many teachers feel nervous their entire career, not just their first year. The best way to dissipate this nervousness is to be prepared (or even overprepared). Consider more tasks to accomplish the first day or two than you believe will be possible to complete. Consider the topics that are most important to cover, then add a few more.

> *I'm getting nervous about the first day. Is this normal?*
>
> **Heather**

Students will have fears on the first day as well. They have no idea what to expect from you. Stand at the door as they enter your classroom and welcome them to your class. Look happy to see each of them. If you have learned any names, use names when greeting the students. Make them feel comfortable.

Try to get rested before you begin the first day. Expect to feel exhausted at the end of this day and every day for the next week or so. In this new routine, you will expend a lot of energy not only working with your students but also in preparing for them each day.

The First Day Celebration

The first day is the most important day of the school year. This is the day you will set the tone and let your students know what to anticipate for the coming year. It is also the day you begin to establish your reputation as a teacher. You cannot be overprepared.

Find out what the school's schedule and procedures are for the first day. Will there be a schoolwide assembly or an extended homeroom period? If so, how long will the class periods be?

> *What should I do during the first class period? Will I have enough time to go over everything?*
>
> **Tanya**

> I have had the same dream every year for 30 years the night before the first day of school. I dream that I am in front of the class the first day in my nightgown. I know why I have this dream—it's because I'm worried about being prepared for my students.
>
> —Sharon, grade 5 teacher

On the first day, you should not focus on a list of rules and regulations. The day should be a celebratory occasion. You may begin your first day with the first lesson of the year, or you may find there are so many things you want to do with your students (some of which could be required by the administration) that your first lesson will take place the following day.

Give students something to look forward to. If you are in a lab setting, create displays of interesting science equipment they will use during the year. You may not have anything accumulated yet, but in the future you will be able to display student work from previous years—the more interesting and creative, the better. Celebrate what the year in your science class will provide for your students.

- ❐ Introduce yourself. The students may know one another, but they don't know you. You should not take the entire time to tell the class about yourself, but you should let them know where you went to college, where you are from, what wonderful things you have heard about them, the positive things you have heard about the school, how much you enjoy learning and doing science, some interesting science-related experiences you've had, and why you selected science teaching as your career. Exhibit the passion and enthusiasm that made you want to be a science teacher.

- ❐ Assure students that they can be successful in your class. Don't insinuate that it will be easy to do well, but emphasize that with work and dedication, everyone will be successful. You may not have success stories to share yet, but be sure to include them in future years.

- ❐ Be confident in yourself and show students that you know what you are doing. Project your knowledge of the science content as well as how to present it. (→ See Chapter 6, "Your Attitude Matters.")

- ❐ Discipline will probably not be an issue the first day. Most students are on their best behavior initially; some teachers say they are sizing you up to see what they can get away with. But if there is a discipline issue, be sure to deal with it. Remember that you are setting the tone for the entire year. (→ See Chapter 4 for more on classroom climate.)

- ❐ Establish an atmosphere that is both serious and fun. Be sure students know there will be rules to follow but that all rules are for the purpose of providing them with a safe environment that will support their learning. There may be several rules to share this first day, such as those dictated by the school concerning tardiness to class, but this is not the day to overwhelm students with rules. Don't try to share every safety rule with them on the first day. (→ See Chapter 5, "Safety in the Laboratory.")

- ❐ Consider a quick hands-on science activity, demonstration, or discrepant event to engage the students. Use it at the end of class time to have them leaving your classroom with the feeling of anticipation for the rest of the year. Or end the class with a funny story. Have them leave your room with an upbeat feeling.

First Day Checklist

Be prepared with these materials:

- ❐ Copy of class lists
- ❐ Bell schedule posted

- ☐ Additional notices and documents from the front office posted or ready to hand out
- ☐ Safety equipment in place
- ☐ All supplies ready
- ☐ Paper and pencils for students who did not come prepared
- ☐ Something nutritious to eat to get you through the day
- ☐ Comfortable, professional clothes and shoes
- ☐ Lesson plan for the day
- ☐ Enough chairs and materials for each student
- ☐ Your name written carefully on the board

Plan to do nothing socially tonight or the rest of the week and get lots of rest. Breathe deep, relax, and enjoy the day!

> One of the things I promise my students on the first day is that I will do anything I can to help them in any way. The harder they work, the harder I work to help.
>
> —Dwayne, grade 9 science teacher

First Week Orientation

Set the stage during the first week. Provide students with a clear concept of what will occur every day in your class. They need to know they can expect specific classroom characteristics such as fairness, learning opportunities, engaging lessons, interaction with their peers, a caring teacher, support, and understanding. During the first week, you should aim to accomplish the following tasks:

- ☐ Introduce your website to your class, if you have one.
- ☐ Provide the class with a syllabus or list of major science concepts they will learn. (→ See Online Appendixes 3.1a–e for sample syllabi.)
- ☐ Explain where they can find things in the room that they will need.
- ☐ Gradually introduce basic routines and rules that allow all students to learn.
- ☐ Explain and provide a safety contract that students will sign and return. (→ See Chapter 5, "Safety in the Laboratory.")
- ☐ Introduce your homework policy and what you expect from students for makeup work.
- ☐ Explain how students can contact you if they need help and inform them of your office hours or times when they can see you to discuss their work.
- ☐ Stress student routines that will be followed in class.
- ☐ Establish a climate that promotes work by individuals and groups. (→ See Chapter 4, "Creating an Environment for Learning.")

Getting Organized

Students will know if you are organized. It's particularly important during the first few weeks to have everything ready for students as they walk in the door. Later, you may engage some of them in setting up materials, distributing items, or collecting things from others. But initially, you need to have all papers, materials, and plans well prepared.

Many teachers find a seating chart beneficial in creating an atmosphere of organization. A seating chart can benefit students and your instruction in several ways:

> Consistency is key. Most students perform best with consistency in expectations, schedules, and processes used in class. This is especially true for students with learning disabilities.
>
> —Shayna, special education teacher

- There will be no argument about who sits where.
- Students who have difficulty focusing and staying on task can be placed in a location in the room where you will have quick access to them and can provide them with on-task behavior suggestions.
- Students with special academic needs can be seated with others who are supportive and in a location you can easily access.
- It will be easy for you to take attendance simply by spotting empty seats and knowing who is missing.
- You will be able to learn student names more quickly and can remind yourself of a name if you are having difficulty.
- You will be able to give students an opportunity to work with a variety of people.
- Lab partners and teams can be selected based on student strengths and needs.
- Students will have a clear message about who is in charge of the class. (→ See Chapter 4 for more on classroom management.)

Getting to Know Your Students

When students are asked about the most important characteristics of a great teacher, the one item that is on nearly all lists is "The teacher knows me and cares about me."

Sherrie

I'm learning the names of my students but I want to really get to know them. Since I'm new to the community, I'm challenged to know their interests and activities. How can I accomplish this in a timely manner?

There are several strategies you can use to learn the names of students quickly.

- If your school has a yearbook, get a copy from the previous year and look up your students. If you don't have a large number of students, you can also look at their cumulative or online folders to see their pictures.
- Make a seating chart.
- If your students don't know one another, play a name game to start the first few classes.
- While students are working and you are helping them, look at their names on their papers or notebook covers.

- Use students' names often in class. "That's a good idea, Otis" or "What do you think of that, Stephanie?" are ways to help you anchor your learning of names and also let students know you are getting to know them.

Getting to know students really goes beyond simply learning their names. You can learn other academic information about students by reviewing their cumulative folders and IEPs. But other information may be harder to find. The time to start gathering information is the first week of school.

- Some information about individual students can be found in the yearbook, as you see them pictured in photos of teams and clubs.
- Ask students or parents to complete an information questionnaire. You could also use an index card or online tool to gather information about students' interests and previous experiences. See the online resources for a sample to get you started. (→ See Online Appendixes 3.2 and 3.3 for sample questionnaires.)
- Stand in the hall in the morning and/or between classes and greet students. Encourage more conversations as you see students each day.
- Get to know students in a different setting than the classroom by attending concerts, sporting events, plays, and other special events at school and in the community.
- Consider having lunch with students or chatting with them in the lunch line.

> It's easy to connect with the students who demand our attention: the hand-raisers, the outgoing personalities, those who are genuinely interested in science, and those who use negative behaviors as attention-grabbers. Getting to know every student is a challenge but it is one of the most important things we can do as teachers.
>
> —Joclyn, grade 7 science teacher

Motivating Students

The first day of school is the best time to begin developing a positive self-image for individuals and groups. When students begin to think of themselves in a negative way, it's almost impossible to change their opinion. Thus, it's important to praise and reinforce the positive things that occur in your class. At the same time, it's important to not give false praise or overpraise students. They have excellent radar and will know if praise is phony or contrived.

- If you sense a negative self-worth on the part of a student, group, or entire class, let them know you don't agree with it.
- Praise positive attributes such as friendliness, creative thinking, cooperation, politeness, motivation, and caring. Then be more specific and connect the attributes to lessons. (→ See Chapter 8 for more on providing informative feedback.)
- You may find that some students do not respond well to public praise. A brief nod or quiet comment may be more appropriate.
- A quick note telling students of something positive they have done will go a long way.
- Students enjoy praise from teachers, but parents seem to appreciate it even more. A positive phone call, postcard, or e-mail to parents can have a major impact on student learning. Many parents have received phone calls

> A positive comment to a parent can be the highlight of a child's day.
>
> —Shayna, special education teacher

only when there is a problem, so they welcome the good news, which is readily passed on to their child. (→ See Chapter 10, "Parent as Partners.")

- As you plan lessons, consider how you might differentiate them to provide opportunities for all students to be successful. (→ See Chapter 7 for more on differentiation and motivating your class.)

Time Management

What should I do if I have planned a lesson that I thought would take the entire class time but I have time left at the end of the period?

Alberto

It's certain that you have heard this previously: You should overplan for your classes. Have more materials and ideas for any block of time than you believe students will require. Even given that, there will still be times when you have more time left over at the end of class. This is the 5–10 minutes that is not enough time to begin the next lesson but too much time to have students idle, which provides opportunities for misbehavior. Be prepared with an extension of the lesson, such as any of the following suggestions for assignments for students:

- An open-ended question about a topic you've been covering that students will hand in when the bell rings
- A question that ties together several ideas you have been studying or applies the work of the day to a different situation
- "What if" questions that encourage critical thinking about the subject you are studying
- A problem that students can pair-and-share
- Simulations or brief video segments related to the lesson
- A "bell-ringer" (→ See Chapter 7 for more on class starters and wrap-up and Chapter 4, "Creating an Environment for Learning.")

Your Professional Appearance

Much of my clothing consists of the jeans and T-shirts I wore to classes. Can I wear that type of clothing while teaching?

Jason

You must separate your leisure appearance from how you want to be perceived as a professional. It's important to project a professional image while at school. If you can create a strong image of yourself as a teacher, your students will respond with respect, as will other teachers and administrators.

You are an adult and a professional. Schools have dress codes or various expectations for the appearance of faculty members. As a first-year teacher, it would be wise to step it up a notch. Don't dress too casually or in styles that are more appropriate for teenagers. That does not mean you must spend a lot of money on a new wardrobe, but try to avoid these errors:

- Dirty or unkempt hair
- Distracting jewelry, slogans, or symbols
- Inappropriate makeup for day wear
- Bad breath, body odor, or too much perfume or aftershave
- Clothing that does not fit properly or cover up appropriately
- Dirty, torn, or crumpled clothing
- Inappropriate footwear (e.g., flip-flops, dirty sneakers)
- Anything that violates the student dress code or lab safety rules, including open-toe shoes in the lab

Clothing cannot make you a better teacher, but your appearance can be a contributing factor to how students perceive you. Your image and reputation begin on the first day of school. Think of the first impression you want to make.

> I keep a pair of my most comfortable, classic shoes at work. If my feet are uncomfortable in my dressier shoes or if I need closed toes to go into a lab, I simply change into my comfortable shoes to get me through the day.
>
> —Lisa, high school principal

Lesson Planning

Immediately begin creating your collection of lesson plans and plan ideas. Your lesson plans should not be set in stone and will not be used in exactly the same manner each year, but having a file of them available will save you a great deal of time and energy in the future. Use three-ring binders, a file cabinet, or your computer to keep all of the materials for each lesson together. Whatever system you select for organizing your materials, be sure they are clearly labeled and in the correct location. You will want to be able to locate specific lessons again next year.

- If this has not already been done for you, begin by organizing the science concepts you will teach in chronological order based on developing conceptual understanding and building knowledge. The new *A Framework for K–12 Science Education: Practices, Crosscutting Concepts, and Core Ideas* (NRC 2011) will help you determine the progression of learning that is important as you consider this order (→ see Resources).
- Determine if your school or department uses a specific model for developing lessons, such as *Understanding by Design* (Wiggins and McTighe 2005), the Madeline Hunter model (Hunter 1994), the BSCS 5E Instructional Model (Bybee 2006), or Marzano's *Art and Science of Teaching* (2007). These resources will provide you with guidelines for preparing your lessons (→ see Resources).
- Consider possible formats for your lesson plans. You may decide that you want to break the activities surrounding a science concept into class session blocks, organize them in a 5E plan, or create an open plan that allows for shifting ideas and activities around within a set time frame.

Be sure to include formative and summative assessments as part of your plan. Your schedule, students' needs, and your personal work style should all be taken into consideration as you formulate your plans.

- Begin gathering information based on science concepts and skills that you want students to develop. Search the web, find print materials, and speak to colleagues to locate investigations, labs, multimedia resources, inquiry topics, readings that are at your students' levels, possible field trip locations, and guest speakers. Join a Listserv to acquire information concerning what other teachers do to address specific science concepts and skills. (→ See Chapter 9, "Creating Professional Development Opportunities.")

- Sort through your collection and organize the selected components in a sequence compatible with the needs of your students. But don't discard the other materials—you may decide to use or modify them as you work through the unit of study.

- Write your lesson plan using all of the selected materials in the format you have chosen.

Conclusion

Subsequent chapters will provide more in-depth information concerning the topics and issues you have encountered during the first weeks of school. If you find there is not enough information in these first three chapters to support your needs, go to the issue-specific chapters now. However, you have plenty to do before delving into the intricacies of each component, and much of the information can wait until you have more time.

Resources *(www.nsta.org/riseandshine)*

Frameworks

Bybee, R. 2006. *The BSCS 5E instructional model: Origins, effectiveness, and application.* Colorado Springs: BSCS. *www.bscs.org/pdf/bscs5eexecsummary.pdf*

Hunter, M. C. 1994. *Enhancing education.* New York: Prentice Hall.

Marzano, R. J. 2007. *Art and science of teaching.* Alexandria, VA: Association for Supervision and Curriculum Design.

National Research Council (NRC). 2011. *A framework for K–12 science education: Practices, crosscutting concepts, and core ideas.* Washington, DC: National Academies Press. *http://books.nap.edu/catalog.php?record_id=13165*

Models

Bybee, R. 2006. *The BSCS 5E instructional model: Origins, effectiveness, and application.* Colorado Springs: BSCS. *www.bscs.org/pdf/bscs5eexecsummary.pdf*

Hunter, M. C. 1994. *Enhancing education.* New York: Prentice Hall.

Marzano, R. J. 2007. *Art and science of teaching.* Alexandria, VA: Association for Supervision and Curriculum Design.

> Reflection is the most important component of lesson planning. At the end of every class, I reflect on what occurred and jot myself a couple of notes concerning how that might impact subsequent lessons for that class or for an individual student.
>
> —Dwayne, grade 9 science teacher

Wiggins, G., and J. McTighe. 2005. *Understanding by design.* 2nd ed. Alexandria, VA: Association for Supervision and Curriculum Design.

Lesson Plan Formats and Templates

Lesson Planning: *www.personal.psu.edu/scs15/idweb/lessonplanning.htm*

Madeline Hunter's Lesson Plan: *http://template.aea267.iowapages.org/lessonplan*

Overview of UbD and the Design Template: *www.grantwiggins.org/documents/UbDQuikvue1005.pdf*

Online Appendixes

3.1a Sample Sixth-Grade Syllabus

3.1b Sample Seventh-Grade Syllabus

3.1c Sample Physics Syllabus

3.1d Sample Honors Chemistry Syllabus

3.1e Sample Earth Science Syllabus

3.2 Student Questionnaire

3.3 Parent Questionnaire

CHAPTER 4
CREATING AN ENVIRONMENT FOR LEARNING

Dear Ms. Mentor,

Alberto *When I have a class discussion, it is dominated by a few students and no one else raises a hand. How can I encourage more students to participate?*

Dear Alberto,

Every teacher has had class discussions turn into seminars with a few students while the others watch. A well-crafted discussion involves student-to-student as well as teacher-to-student conversations. However, students may have learned that if they don't raise their hands, the teacher won't call on them or that some students will raise their hands immediately and monopolize the teacher's attention.

At first, students may rebel against changing these traditions, so explain the reasons for using new strategies. While students may certainly raise their hands, you reserve the right to call on others because you're interested in what everyone has to say. You want to encourage more in-depth thinking, get a variety of viewpoints, assess student learning informally, and create a classroom environment where everyone's questions and contributions are valued.

To call on students randomly or equitably, pick from a set of cards with students' names on them. It is certainly acceptable to call on students who raise their hands too.

For questions requiring short answers, ask students to hold up individual whiteboards or pieces of paper with their responses, give a thumbs-up, down, or sideways signal, or use electronic response systems to encourage participation and serve as a formative assessment strategy. But I assume by "discussion," you mean more than a question-and-answer drill. You should also include higher-level questions or prompts to focus the discussion. Provide informative feedback during the discussion, but don't monopolize the discussion yourself.

Another effective way to encourage discussions is "wait time." After you pose a question or topic, pause four or five seconds before calling on a student. Some students (including those for whom English is their second language) may need time to compose their thoughts. Waiting is hard for teachers to do, but the "dead air" is actually thinking time, and research has shown that the students' responses are often at a higher level of complexity after a waiting period. After a student's response, use more wait time. During these few seconds, the student may elaborate on the response, or another student may contribute. Before you respond, call on other students: "Do you have anything to add?" or "Do you agree or disagree?" To acknowledge those who did raise their hands, you can say, "I noticed your hand was up too. What were you going to say?"

How should you respond if you call on someone involuntarily who answers incorrectly or with "I don't know"? Ask some probing questions for clarification (perhaps the student did not hear the question). Rephrase the question with different vocabulary, or smile and say "OK, I'll come back to you later." Be sure to do so.

It may take a while for you and the students to adapt to a different kind of class discussion, so give yourself time to try new strategies and model the type of conversations you expect from the students.

—Ms. Mentor

IN STRUCTURING A learning environment, several terms are often used interchangeably. These terms (Rothstein-Fisch and Trumbull 2008) describe an interrelated set of teacher practices:

- *Classroom management:* the set of expectations, routines, and rules established to ensure a positive, safe learning environment
- *Classroom organization:* the efficient use of time, space, and materials to promote learning
- *Discipline:* actions taken by the teacher to control or correct student behavior

Think of your classroom as an ecosystem—a set of interconnected components such as the classroom itself, the available resources, and the people who inhabit it. When these components are working well together, learning can be a joyous, exciting adventure. When one or more components break down, the entire system can be affected. With careful planning, organization, and monitoring, you can develop an effective system for you and your students.

Classroom Management

In my methods class, I learned a lot about academic learning goals and how to attain them. But where do I start helping students meet the behavioral expectations I have for my classroom?

Sherrie

You'll find that most students want some structure, even though they may not admit it. Good classroom management fosters student self-discipline if students have an understanding of (and input into) the expectations, routines, and rules.

Expectations

In addition to learning goals, you should establish expectations for students (and yourself) with regard to collaboration, scholarship, participation, decorum, and self-discipline. These expectations will be the framework for the routines and rules in the classroom. Expectations can include statements such as the following:

- Class participation is important for learning.
- Everyone will be treated with respect and courtesy.
- Everyone must come to class prepared and ready to learn.

Discuss your expectations, post them on the wall, include them in the syllabus or newsletter, and ask the students to put them in their notebooks. Model the behavior you expect from students related to these expectations. If you want students to be polite, you must be polite. Model other behaviors such as commitment, promptness, enthusiasm for learning, active listening, anger control, consideration for others, honesty, and paying attention (McLeod, Fisher, and Hoover 2003). (→ See Chapter 6 for more on the qualities of an effective teacher.) During the year, you can modify your expectations with student input. But remember that you are the adult in the classroom, and what happens there is ultimately your responsibility.

You also communicate your expectations in the type of assignments you give, how they are structured and assessed, and the feedback you provide. Giving students difficult tasks with little support is not a sign of rigor. It will lead to frustration (for both you and the students). Students enjoy and learn from challenges when they have or learn the tools and skills to meet the challenge and if the topic is relevant and the learning activities are interesting. Students also

Try to maintain your sense of humor and avoid humiliation, sarcasm, or foul language—students get enough of these in other situations.

—Ty, middle school principal

like choices, whether in terms of content or learning activities. (See Chapter 7, "Teaching Strategies.")

Routines

Some classrooms seem to be more orderly than others. How do the teachers maintain order?

Heather

Having a set of routines can help students meet your expectations. These routines describe a desired way to perform everyday tasks. Establishing routines for the beginning and end of class (as well as for transitions between activities) frees your time for learning activities rather than discipline or logistical issues.

Visualize what a class activity should look like. In your mind, go in slow motion through the activity and focus on what the students should be doing to accomplish the task in an orderly, timely, and safe manner. Having routines for tasks such as these can maximize learning time:

- What to do when entering or leaving the room
- Where to place book bags and other materials upon entering the room
- How and where to get notebooks and other class supplies
- Where to look for posted assignments
- Where to place homework and/or pick up printed assignments
- How to access and return lab equipment
- How to turn in assignments
- How and when to ask permission to leave the classroom for the restroom or nurse (See Pappalardo 2011 in Resources for suggestions.)
- How to get extra help
- How to clean up the lab
- When students should stop whatever they are doing and listen
- What students should do when they complete the work assigned for class that day
- When it is appropriate to begin cleaning and/or packing up at the end of class

At first, be explicit with routines. Give directions verbally, model them yourself, and provide opportunities for practice. It's important to distinguish between routines and regimentation. Regimentation occurs when the teacher continually tells students exactly what to do and when to do it. In a classroom in which the students have internalized the routines, however, the students know what to do even if the teacher is not in the room. The teacher's routines have helped the students move from obedience or compliance to responsibility and self-discipline. Although some of your routines could eventually be modified

> You'll know when students have internalized the routines. The class can function even when you have a substitute.
>
> —Lisa, high school principal

with input from your students, others may be schoolwide with no room for negotiation (e.g., fire drills).

Rules for Student Behavior

What kind of rules should I establish?

Jason

Rules are requirements related to safety (both physical and intellectual) and maintaining order. For example, your lab safety contract contains rules about wearing goggles. (→ See Chapter 5 for more on safety contracts and student orientation.) Your school has rules about hall traffic and accessing lockers. You may have classroom rules about keeping the aisles clear or speaking out of turn.

As with routines, the ultimate goal of rules is self-discipline: Students will know what is required and have the skills to meet these requirements. Safety rules should be posted, and a copy of the safety contract should be in each student's notebook. Rather than having a lengthy list of rules that could easily be ignored, post the most important rules. Your rules should relate to your expectations and routines. An example of this relationship would be as follows:

- Expectation: Students will work safely in the lab.
- Routine: One team member will get the goggles from the storage area before the team starts the activity. At the end of the period, that student will return the goggles to the designated place.
- Rule: All students must wear eye protection when directed by the teacher.

Some rules are hard and fast; others could have levels of interpretation. Choose your battles when you decide on non-negotiable class rules. For example, a student who is late once should not have the same consequence as one who is habitually late.

You probably remember teachers who seemed to have eyes in the back of their heads. During class, the best way to ensure that students are learning the routines and following the rules is to be aware of what is going on. (See p. 43 for more on dealing with off-task or disruptive behavior.)

Some teachers have an elaborate reward system for students who follow the routines and obey the rules. Others note that if students understand the rationale and have input into the rules, they won't need extrinsic reinforcements unrelated to the behavior (e.g., stickers, candy, points, coupons). Students do appreciate compliments, but some might not like public recognition. A smile, nod, or quiet "thank you" may be appropriate.

When students are following the routines or rules, frame your compliments in *you* rather than *I* statements (McLeod, Fisher, and Hoover 2003). Saying "I like how you're talking quietly" implies that the student's' role is compliance or

Along with my classroom routines and rules, I also set targets. I choose a problem I want to solve, establish the target, and provide a reward for the class when the target is reached. No papers without student names for two weeks, no one late to class for a week, all labs cleaned up by the time the bell rings for a week ... [these] are all targets I have set and rewarded.

—Dale, grade 3 teacher

pleasing the teacher. "When you're talking quietly, as you are now, it's easier to think and work" shows students the positive results of their behavior.

Interruptions and Distractions

Despite your established routines, there will be interruptions and distractions that students will have to learn to handle. The effects can be minimized with planning and preparation:

- Schools are required to conduct periodic drills requiring students and teacher to evacuate the room. ($\rightarrow$ See Chapter 5 for more on challenging circumstances.)
- Turn off your personal cell phone during class (you'll be a role model as you ask students to do the same). Turn off any audible alarms that could be distracting.
- You can't control announcements over a public address system. Have a signal to get students back on task afterward.
- Put a "Learning in Progress" sign outside your room, along with a note to slide memos under the door.
- After a while, students will get used to having visitors such as principals on walk-throughs. Assign a student who sits near the door to answer the door to greet visitors.
- During class, students may need to leave the room to take medications or visit the restroom. Establish rules about leaving the room. However, you may find that when students are engaged in an activity, the restroom requests decrease.
- Sometimes students will be called from your class to an assembly or other event. Ask about where your students should sit and whether they should sit together as a class.

Preparing for a Substitute

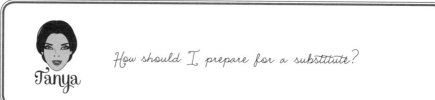

Tanya

How should I prepare for a substitute?

Eventually, you'll need to use a sick day or have an opportunity to attend a workshop or meeting during the school day. Someone will have to cover your classes, whether it's a substitute or a colleague. Students may try to engage in unacceptable behavior when you're out. Before your first absence, discuss how your expectations will still be in place. Remind them that the usual routines and rules should be followed and that the sub will provide a report.

If you know in advance when you'll be out and who the sub will be, you can prepare class activities appropriate for his or her knowledge and skills. But sometimes, as in the case of illness, you don't have the opportunity to create

Emergency days (e.g., weather-related delays and cancellations or other unanticipated events in the community) affect everyone and most will need to be made up (although extra days at the end of the year are not as productive). Some teachers post activities on their websites for these days.

—Ty, middle school principal

detailed plans. Having an up-to-date and available sub folder can be a lifesaver for both you and the sub. This folder should include the following information:

- ❏ A seating chart for each period with the students' first and last names
- ❏ Bell schedules, emergency routines (e.g., fire drill directions), a map of the school noting the location of your room and the faculty room, the name of a nearby teacher who can assist with questions or problems, and directions on how to contact the office
- ❏ The syllabus for each course you teach as an overview of the content and expectations
- ❏ A note with any routines that should be followed at the beginning and end of the day and during each period (e.g., taking attendance)
- ❏ A form for the sub to leave a status report of what was accomplished during each class, along with any issues, problems, success stories, or suggestions
- ❏ Several days' worth of activities that relate to the learning goals for your course (→ see Chapter 7 for more on preparing for a substitute)

Even if you're positive the sub is credentialed in science and familiar with laboratory routines and safety rules, don't ask the sub to do a lab investigation with the potential for student injury, such as those requiring chemicals, live specimens, flames, projectiles, or heat sources.

If the substitute did not follow your plans or allowed students to behave in unacceptable or unsafe ways, you have the responsibility to share this information with your principal. And if the sub did an exemplary job, tell the principal so that this person can be called again for your class. (→ See Online Appendix 4.1, "For the Substitute.")

> I designate a student in each class as a "techie" to assist substitutes with any technology issues.
>
> —Pat, grade 11 science teacher

Classroom Organization

Did you ever visit a classroom where everything seemed to move like clockwork? Or one that followed the adage "a place for everything and everything in its place" This level of organization did not happen overnight. The teacher designed the classroom for the efficient and effective use of space.

Students need a safe physical environment, with classroom and lab spaces that are conducive to learning and free from hazards. As you organize space and materials, experiment with ways to ensure easy and safe movement within the classroom, orderly entry into and exit from the room, access to safety equipment and class supplies, and teacher proximity to assist students and deter undesirable behavior.

Think about your room as having several "centers":

- Lab area (→ see Chapter 5 for more on your classroom or lab)
- Office center with class supplies, extra textbooks, reading material, and places for students to submit assignments and store their notebooks

- Technology center with desktop computers, the laptop cart, printers, and other electronics
- Interest centers with objects or materials related to the topic for students to explore when other assignments are complete
- A study center with carrels for students doing makeup work or those who need fewer distractions
- Operations center (your desk), which is off-limits to students

Safety is a priority. If you're in a typical lab, you probably have an area with lab tables and a classroom section with individual desks or small tables. This area is probably not as large as a regular classroom, so your options for arranging desks are more limited. Whatever arrangement(s) you use, be sure all students can enter and exit the classroom efficiently and backpacks, electrical cords, and other materials can be kept out of the walkways.

Determine the focal point of the classroom (e.g., whiteboard or projection screen, demonstration table) and be sure that your seating arrangements do not require some students to have their backs to the focal point. If space is tight, count the number of students in your largest class assigned to the room, add one or two to allow for move-ins, and ask if extra desks can be stored elsewhere.

Review students' individual education plans to determine any special seating requirements. Make sure that any new arrangements can accommodate the visual, auditory, and physical needs of your students, as well as any assistive technologies or devices they use.

What is the best way to arrange the seating in my room?

Alberto

Your seating arrangement should enhance the learning process. At the beginning of the year, you probably set up a default seating arrangement (→ see Chapter 2 for more on the classroom or lab arrangement). As the year progresses, experiment with different seating arrangements as you learn more about your students and try different instructional strategies. Each seating arrangement has advantages and disadvantages. Assign seats in your default arrangement to establish your routines. Then change the seating arrangement to match the type of learning activity (see Resources).

- Traditional rows of desks or tables facing the focal point are often used for teacher-centered activities (lecturing, giving directions, or presenting on the whiteboard) or independent activities (tests, silent reading). Many teachers use this arrangement as the default. However, there are dead zones in the corners and the back of the room; students in the front center also are more likely to get your attention. While this arrangement minimizes distractions, it also limits student-to-student discussions because students are looking at the backs of other students.

- A U-shaped arrangement fosters student-to-student discussions within a large group. This is also useful for teacher-centered presentations, as you can maintain eye contact with all students. As students work, you can move around the perimeter to monitor and provide assistance. For large-group discussions, you can close the U to make a circle and sit with the students, sending the message that you are part of the discussion. However, this takes up a lot of space, and some students may be easily distracted during independent work.
- For collaborative activities, consider pushing desks together. Pairs of desks are good for turn-and-talk activities, and groups of three or four students are appropriate for cooperative learning. You can also use the lab tables for small-group work, unless equipment and materials are set up for another class. This arrangement could also be distracting during independent work.

You may have a separate office connected to the lab. If not, designate a desk or counter as your personal space for storing extra materials and your own belongings. Establish a rule that your personal space, your computer, and the file cabinets are off-limits to students. Keep anything that includes students' names, your personal electronics, or other valuable or sensitive materials out of sight in a locked drawer.

> I have a teacher's desk in my room to help me stay organized. However, I use the demo table in the front of the room to keep my daily plans, handouts, laptop, and projector. A small table or lectern would work too—just so you don't have to go back and forth to your desk.
>
> —Joclyn, grade 7 science teacher

Classroom Climate

Students need a positive social environment in which they feel intellectually safe—a place where they all feel welcome as learners and their participation will be valued by others. By providing different kinds of learning opportunities during a class period (→ see Chapter 7 for more on motivating your class), you'll increase the chances for students to participate and to be engaged in their learning.

Class Participation

Ms. Mentor's response to the question at the beginning of this chapter has suggestions for getting all students (even the reluctant ones) to participate in a group discussion. Sometimes, however, the opposite happens—too many students try to talk at once. Their enthusiasm should be celebrated, but a few overeager students shouldn't discourage or shout down the ideas of others. If your class expectation is that everyone should be treated with respect and courtesy, then establish a few rules, such as the following:

- Raise your hand.
- Don't interrupt someone else.
- Don't make fun of someone else's answer.

What should I do when students try to interrupt each other?

Sherrie

> I often ask a student to be the class scribe and write on the interactive board during the discussion as another form of participation.
>
> —Dwayne, grade 9 science teacher

Talk to your overeager students privately and individually. "I appreciate your enthusiasm and knowledge. But as the teacher, I have to give everyone a chance to participate. So even if I don't call on you, I still value your ideas and questions." A wink or slight nod in a student's direction will acknowledge waving hands as you call on other students. But make it very clear that any behavior or language belittling other students is unacceptable. You can model appropriate conversations by asking probing follow-up questions and providing constructive feedback.

Sometimes students ask questions or offer comments only tangentially related to the topic (or perhaps totally unrelated). These might be teachable moments worth pursuing. If not, use a section of a bulletin board or wall space as a "parking lot." Ask the student to write the question on a sticky note or index card and add it to the parking lot to be addressed at another time. Revisit the parking lot periodically to look at the topics and respond to them. Then remove the card when the issue is addressed, thanking the student for asking the question earlier.

If a student asks a question and you don't know the answer, the worst thing you can do is make up an answer. It's acceptable (and honest) for a teacher to say, "That's an interesting question, but I'm not sure how to answer it. What do you think? Does anyone else have an idea?" If the question is directly related to the lesson, you could model how you would go about finding information. If it's not related, add it to the parking lot and go on with the lesson. If the student has some extra time, encourage him or her to find information and share with the class.

Academic Integrity

How can I encourage students to turn in original work?

Jason

Another expectation you should have for your students is that they will do their own work. Students may try to get away with turning in a report written by someone else or copied from another source, writing notes on a shirt cuff or a piece of paper to use during a test, sharing the contents of a test, copying assignments, or paraphrasing information without citing sources. High-tech applications make it easy to text answers to others, download complete documents from online sources, access online answers and solutions to textbook review questions and problems, take pictures of a test with a cell phone camera, or store information on handheld devices.

You could assume that students cheat because they are lazy or unmotivated (which may be true in some cases). However, talking with students may uncover some other reasons. Some students fear that their original work will be penalized for being less than perfect. Students have demands on their time (extracurricular activities, jobs, family responsibilities) beyond the school day. They may not see the relevance of the assignment or understand the task. It seems that many students don't know what working independently really means, especially in terms of newer media, and they assume helping (or being helped by) a friend is always acceptable.

Find out if there is a schoolwide policy about academic integrity:

- What is your school's definition of cheating (including examples)?
- How are students and parents informed of the policy (e.g., in the student handbook or on the school's website)?
- How is the policy enforced, and what are the consequences for violating it?

Have a frank discussion with the students about your expectations and what is or is not acceptable in your class. For example, in a cooperative learning situation, students helping each other is desirable; in other situations, such as a test, individual accountability is necessary. Review and provide examples showing the differences between original thoughts and verbatim copying, paraphrasing (using different words), and summarizing (identifying the important concepts). Review copyright guidelines for both text and multimedia that students want to use in their projects ($\rightarrow$ see Resources).

How assignments are structured and assessed can affect the temptation to cheat.

- Do you evaluate the process as well as the correctness of a response?
- Do you demand perfection on every assignment, or is it permissible for students to make mistakes during practice exercises (such as homework) without fear of a failing grade?
- Do you encourage students to submit interim drafts of important writing assignments for your feedback?
- Are your questions easily answered verbatim from web searches, or do they require original thinking?
- Is there flexibility in how students can respond?

Model appropriate behavior yourself. Be sure to cite any sources you use for a handout or worksheet (and credit yourself if it's original). Model how to cite direct quotes and paraphrased or summarized information. Review and model note-taking and study skills. ($\rightarrow$ See Online Appendix 4.2 for suggestions for determining the originality of student work.)

> Should electronic devices be allowed in the schools? There are many creative and legitimate uses of these tools in learning environments. We need to discuss the appropriate uses of these devices in terms of digital literacy and academic integrity.
>
> —Lisa, high school principal

Student Diversity

I have students who are not engaged in our classroom activities. What can I do to get them involved constructively?

— Tanya

Even on the first day of school, you will notice differences in your students. Each student brings a unique combination of knowledge, skills, and experiences to the classroom. As you get to know your students, use your awareness of their differences to enhance student engagement in learning activities.

What you once thought was off-task behavior could perhaps be a different way of thinking. For example, the student staring out the window may indeed be daydreaming—or she could be deep in thought. The students involved in a sidebar conversation might be planning a social event—or they could be talking about a related science concept. The student doodling on a piece of paper may be trying to distract others—or he could be translating written content into a graphic. Before you criticize the behavior and create a discipline event, ask the students about what they're doing.

Special Needs

Talk with special education teachers about the requirements for a student with an IEP (Individualized Education Plan) to become aware of factors such the student's reading level, attention issues, how he or she works with other students, and accommodations for testing. A team made up of a counselor, special education teacher, science teacher, and administrator should determine appropriate placement of these students in a lab setting. The need for special equipment or an aide should also be determined at the time of placement.

Adjust your seating plans for students who have visual, hearing, or orthopedic issues. Make sure that aisles can accommodate wheelchairs or assistive devices.

Socioeconomic Issues

Many students face overwhelming economic and social situations outside of school. These external situations can affect student learning, and many are beyond the control of the teacher. But you can do something about what happens within your classroom.

Students certainly need love, respect, and patience. But if students have not had much success academically, they also need modeling, guided practice, feedback, resources, a positive classroom environment, and opportunities for using inquiry and creativity. High expectations (and a support system), routines, and a positive rapport all contribute to a positive climate for learning.

It's also helpful if you can provide resources that many students take for granted: pencils, paper, time in a computer lab, information about the public library, science reading materials or videos, and a quiet place to read or study.

> Information about students that you get from the special education teacher, nurse, or guidance counselor must be kept confidential.
>
> —Shayna, special education teacher

Dealing With Off-Task or Disruptive Behavior

What are some effective ways to deal with students who disrupt the class?

Sherrie

Despite your efforts to maintain high expectations, plan effective lessons, establish routines, and organize your resources, there will be students who engage in off-task, disruptive, or disrespectful behaviors. The causes often originate outside your classroom—events that happened at home, on the way to school, in the halls, or in another class—but you'll need to have some discipline strategies to deal with the behaviors before they escalate into unsafe conditions.

Generally, you'll find that 70% of your students are cooperative and do not break rules, and 10% are defiant and may have issues well beyond the classroom or conditions that affect with their behavior (you may need outside assistance with these students). The remaining 20% require your guidance to learn the routines and rules in your classroom (Curwin, Mendler, and Mendler 2008).

Ask students individually about off-task behaviors that may be a signal of something else, such as putting his head on a desk ("Are you feeling OK?") or daydreaming ("What are you thinking about?"). If you need everyone's attention, use silence or a predetermined signal rather than raising your voice.

Many disruptions include bullying, name-calling, and teasing. Your intervention should reinforce that this type of behavior is unacceptable in a safe learning environment. (And of course a teacher should never model this type of behavior.) Likewise, when students are engaged in unsafe activities or interrupting other students, you will need to intervene.

Start small with your interventions to get students' attention and refocus their behavior. If you blow up at every disruption, you'll become part of the show:

- Ignore the behavior if it is not actually interfering with the class. Bringing attention to it may cause a greater disruption.
- Try nonverbal responses first—eye contact, proximity, a gesture such as a finger to the lips, or a time-out signal.
- Call on the student by name with a question about the lesson or ask for his or her thoughts on the subject. Use the student's name in a positive way: "Joe, when we're finished with this problem, I'm going to call on you."
- If the student is distracted by an object, remove the object (and return it to the student at an appropriate time).
- State your request for compliance firmly: "Laura, sit at your desk." "Put your goggles on, Anthony." Use eye contact as you address the student.
- Never get into a shouting match or power struggle with a student. No matter what the outcome, you're still the loser. Take the student aside (in the back of the room or the hallway) and talk calmly about the behavior.

> Don't send a child to an administrator as a way of handling simple discipline problems. Attempt to control discipline within your own classroom. In that way you are not relinquishing your authority. Sending a student to the office should be the last intervention you use unless school rules dictate otherwise.
>
> —Sharon, grade 5 teacher

Your reaction should not be more of a distraction than the student's original action.

- Never ask a question if you don't want an answer. If you ask, "How many times have I told you …," it's very tempting for a student to respond as an attention-getter.
- Change the seating arrangement to place the student in a situation with fewer distractions and easier access for you.
- Some students (even older ones) may need a time-out at a table or study carrel or standing in the hall at the door. If this is not allowed in your school, have a reciprocal agreement with a nearby teacher for time-outs.
- Decide on consequences. If a student writes on a desk, he cleans it up. If she takes another student's pencil, she returns it. If students are careless with equipment, they are not allowed to participate for a while, until they understand the acceptable behavior and can follow the rules. Explain and post the consequences for violating your most important rules. For example, detentions could be a consequence for interruptions of class time, giving the offender an opportunity to make up for this time.
- Have the disruptive student sign a behavior contract that includes consequences. Consider sending a copy home to inform the parents, including a description of past behaviors.
- Notify parents or guardians of the behaviors. This may be the last action you will need to take with a student.

Be sure to differentiate between behaviors that are disruptive or destructive and those that are simply annoying. In the latter case, the best response is no response. A student who drops something on the floor to get your attention may cease if you do not react. Keep things in perspective and choose simple solutions. For example, if a student unconsciously taps her pencil while she is thinking, give her a rubber pad to deaden the sound. If a student finds it difficult to sit at the end of the day, encourage him to participate while standing in the back of the room.

Criticize the action, not the student, and try to maintain a sense of dignity (yours and the student's). Regardless of the infraction, don't hold a grudge—let it go and move on. Don't send students to the office for minor misbehaviors. These can and should be handled within the classroom. Use the principal's intervention for major infractions.

However, if the student poses a physical threat to you, himself or herself, or other students, you will need assistance. Call the office and another teacher immediately for assistance. Keep your distance when anger (yours or the student's) is part of the situation. A student's defiance or uncontrollable anger is sometimes part of a larger issue and usual interventions may not work. Discuss the situation with the principal, special education teacher, school nurse, or guidance counselor to determine the best course of action.

Some schools have a discipline form that teachers are expected to fill out to document events. If your school does not have such a form, it is still a good idea to document what the student did, the circumstances around the behavior, who else was involved, what you did in response, if and how the situation was

> One of my "aha" moments came when I realized that students do not necessarily think about or respond to things the same way I do. When I varied my class activities, many so-called "discipline" problems disappeared.
>
> —Pat, grade 11 science teacher

resolved, and any further steps that should be taken (e.g., notifying the principal, calling the parents).

Conclusion

Experienced teachers have learned that preventing discipline problems is better than using class time to respond to them. You may have observed (or experienced) classrooms that were sterile, joyless, and regimented. Your science classroom should be a stimulating place where you and your students can focus on activities to explore and learn. By establishing routines, being organized, and using interesting activities with relevant content, teachers can work with students to create an engaging learning environment (with a minimum number of rules and disruptions).

Resources *(www.nsta.org/riseandshine)*

Discipline

Boynton, M., and C. Boynton. 2005. *The educator's guide to preventing and solving discipline problems.* Alexandria, VA: Association for Supervision and Curriculum Development.

Curwin, R. L., A. N. Mendler, and B. D. Mendler. 2008. *Discipline with dignity.* 3rd ed. Alexandria, VA: Association for Supervision and Curriculum Development.

Classroom Management

Himmele, P., and W. Himmele. 2011. *Total participation techniques: Making every student an active learner.* Alexandria, VA: Association for Supervision and Curriculum Development.

Marzano, R. 2003. *Classroom management that works.* Alexandria, VA: Association for Supervision and Curriculum Development.

McLeod, J., J. Fisher, and G. Hoover. 2003. *The key elements of classroom management.* Alexandria, VA: Association for Supervision and Curriculum Development.

Pappalardo, G. 2011. Classroom management strategies for elementary teachers. Edutopia. *www.edutopia.org/blog/classroom-management-strategies-elementary-teacher.* A blog entry that takes a humorous look at students' needs for going to the nurse, pencil sharpening, and other behaviors.

Rothstein-Fisch, C., and E. Trumbull. 2008. *Managing diverse classrooms.* Alexandria, VA: Association for Supervision and Curriculum Development.

Classroom Design and Seating Arrangements

Classroom Architect: *http://classroom.4teachers.org.* A floor plan template to be filled in with items you have in your classroom

Classroom Design: Layout: *http://ethemes.missouri.edu/themes/1435.* Links to several resources for designing and arranging classrooms

Classroom Set-Up Tool: *http://teacher.scholastic.com/tools/class_setup.* A tool that allows you to design your floor plan and determine placement of furniture and materials

Motz, L. L., J. T. Biehle, and S. S. West. 2007. *NSTA guide to planning school science facilities.* 2nd ed. Arlington, VA: NSTA Press.

Organizing Your Classroom: *http://www2.scholastic.com/browse/collection.jsp?id=329.* Suggestions for setting up learning centers and reducing clutter

Academic Integrity

Academic Integrity Policies From Selected Schools: *www.ethicsed.org/programs/integrity-works/policies.htm*

Copyright Advisory Network: *http://librarycopyright.net/wordpress/?page_id=10*

Educational Tips on Plagiarism Prevention: *www.plagiarism.org/plag_article_educational_tips_on_plagiarism_prevention.html*

John F. Kennedy High School (Granada Hills, CA) Academic Integrity Policy: *www.jfkcougars.org/academic_integrity_policy.jsp*

Online Appendixes

4.1 For the Substitute
4.2 Determining the Originality of Student Work

CHAPTER 5
SAFETY IN THE LABORATORY

Heather

Dear Ms. Mentor,

My students want to have animals in the classroom. Is that a good idea?

Dear Heather,

Living things in a science classroom add many teachable moments, but there are safety issues to consider. Begin by checking on your school's regulations about keeping animals and plants in the classroom. You don't want venomous animals, ones that make distracting noises, or ones that require highly controlled environments. Before you make any decisions, find out if any students have allergies to hair, fur, feathers, or bedding materials. Wild animals such as chipmunks or songbirds do not belong in the classroom (and possessing them may be in violation of state or local game laws). Aquariums and small rodents such as gerbils, mice, or hamsters are popular in classrooms. Teachers also recommend hissing cockroaches, snakes (such as ball pythons or corn snakes), and other "herps." Get animals from a reputable pet shop or other providers (including rescue organizations) that can advise you and the students on caring for the animals. Never release classroom pets (or their offspring) into the wild.

There are many opportunities for inquiry with plants and terrariums, especially if students start them from seeds or clippings. Choose plants that are not toxic to humans and use sterilized potting soil to reduce mold. Be sure to have hand-washing facilities nearby if students touch animals, soil, or plants.

There are other practical and logistical issues:

- Who will feed the animals or water the plants on weekends or long breaks?
- How much does the temperature fluctuate in your classroom?
- Do the custodians use cleaning chemicals or pesticides that may be harmful to animals and plants?
- Do you have secure containers or cages for the animals?

Set up a schedule for feeding and caring for the living things, involving students (under supervision) when possible. Don't send animals home with students unless you are personally acquainted with the parents and know the student and parents could properly care for the animals. Get written permission from the parents and include a fact sheet about the care and feeding of the animal.

Students like to share what they find, but set some guidelines as to what they can bring into the classroom. Include these in the safety contract at the beginning of the year so that parents are also aware. This would include "rescuing" baby animals, especially rabbits and birds. Commend students for their concern, but urge them not to remove animals from their surroundings. Contact your state's game commission, park rangers, or animal control agency to learn about any permits or licenses you would need to collect or possess roadkill or other specimens from the wild (including bones and feathers).

Check with state or local regulations and school policy to see if bringing pets to school is permissible and what would be required in terms of licenses or vaccinations. Even pets that are well mannered at home can react negatively in unfamiliar settings. Exceptions, of course, must be made for students who require assistance dogs.

—Ms. Mentor

WHEN YOU WERE student teaching or doing an internship, your cooperating teacher already had lab routines and rules in place. But now you're in charge! You must be proactive about student safety during laboratory activities. You can't claim ignorance and use the excuse of being a new teacher.

The purpose of this chapter is to raise your awareness of safety in the science classroom. This chapter is not meant to be a comprehensive guide to safety. Publications such as NSTA's *Exploring Safely* (elementary), *Inquiring Safely* (middle school), and *Investigating Safely* (high school) are a wealth of information and should be in your school or personal library. NSTA also has position papers related to student lab work and safety, as well as a Safety in the Science Classroom portal. The Council for State Science Supervisors (CSSS), the National Science Education Leadership Association (NSELA), and other state and national science education associations also provide information concerning safety. (→ See Resources for helpful links.)

The Role of the Science Teacher in Safety

The safety issues scare me, especially with younger students. Who can give me advice?

Alberto

You may have read horror stories about science labs, from careless mistakes or oversights to deliberate mischief and vandalism. These events can have serious consequences for student safety (and the career of the science teacher). Things you may have found amusing when you were a student are different from your perspective as a teacher.

As a science teacher, you have responsibilities beyond those of other teachers. Your students will use materials, equipment, and procedures that could be hazardous, and it's your responsibility to ensure that students are aware of and use proper precautions and safe routines. You're also responsible for maintaining inventories and handling and storing materials and equipment safely.

You may have walked into a situation where your predecessor was organized and aware of safety considerations—or not. Whatever the situation, it's now yours. In addition to student safety, you must also consider your own safety and that of classroom visitors (custodians, aides, observers, administrators).

Find out who is the designated safety officer in your school or district. This could be the department chair or someone on the facilities or maintenance staff. This officer is charged with keeping everyone aware of safety regulations. The officer should make at least one visit each year to your lab to check for compliance with regulations and determine if safety equipment is in working order and available to you and your students. The officer should have copies of the local and state laws and guidelines on topics such as chemical safety and disposal (including a master set of Material Safety Data Sheets [MSDS]), lab and storeroom security, health and occupancy regulations, fire codes, and possession of live animals. Ask the safety officer about the protocol for reporting spills, accidents, or missing equipment.

The special education faculty, school nurse, and guidance counselors should have information on students who require accommodations for disabilities and who have allergies or behavioral issues that could affect their participation in lab activities. A team made up of a counselor, special education teacher, science teacher, and administrator should determine appropriate placement of these students in a lab setting. The need for special equipment or an aide should also be determined at the time of placement.

Safety should be a topic in programs for new teachers. The science department chair should have safety as an ongoing topic at meetings and professional development events. But even if it is not, you're still responsible for the safety of your students.

> Although MSDS documents can be accessed electronically, we have a binder with the current sheets readily available to the science teachers.
>
> —Richard, science department chair

Your Classroom or Lab

What should I check for in my room before conducting my first lab?

Jason

Although you toured your classroom or lab when you were hired, before you do your first activity, take time for a more thorough inspection. The facilities you have will influence the types of activities your students can safely do and the security practices and routines you'll need to put in place.

- A classroom with separate lab tables (in another section of the room or on the perimeter) is a common configuration. The separate tables make it easier to keep equipment and materials in place and away from student horseplay. However, you'll need to establish routines for students to move back and forth between the two areas in a safe and orderly fashion. During lab activities, you should be able to supervise students in both sections of the room.
- A combination classroom and lab in which student tables double as lab stations poses some concerns. There is less movement in the classroom between activities, but it's harder to go over safety procedures before an activity when the materials are right on the table and students can "explore" them. Students may be tempted to play with the electrical outlets, water faucets, or gas jets at the tables.
- Being assigned to a regular classroom for all or some of your classes can be a huge challenge for a science teacher. Unless you also have access to a lab on some days, the activities that can be done safely will be limited. (See Challenging Circumstances later in this chapter.)

Your classroom may also have doors that connect to another classroom, a lab storage room, a prep room, a mini lab for projects and makeup work, or an office. The doors to storage and prep rooms should always be locked, and students should not be in these areas, even with your permission or supervision. Doors to a mini lab, an adjoining classroom, and your office should be locked when you are not in the room.

As you consider your curriculum and the types of activities that students may undertake, do an inventory of the room:

- ☐ Check the utilities. Note the locations of electrical outlets. Avoid using long extension cords or outlet multipliers. If there is gas in the room, test the gas jets. Find out where the master valve is and keep the gas turned off when not in use. Report the location of any leaky faucets or nonfunctioning gas jets and electrical outlets to the maintenance staff.
- ☐ All science labs require two exits. If you do not have two ways to

exit your room, determine if there is another way to leave in case of emergency. On the first floor, you may have windows that provide that exit. If another exit is not obvious, ask your department chair or principal how to exit. Don't assume that you may use a prep room as an exit, even if it has a door to the hallway.

❏ Put a sign on appliances such as a dishwasher or refrigerator that they are to be used only for science-related materials (e.g., not for washing coffee mugs or storing lunches or treats).

❏ If the room has an eyewash station, fire blanket, and emergency shower, be sure they are functional and accessible to the students. Look at the date on the fire extinguisher for a recent inspection and read the directions for its use. Try out the fume hood. Report any malfunctions to the safety officer.

❏ Put cleanup materials in accessible locations: a dustpan, paper towels, hand soap, and a box to dispose of broken glass or other sharp objects.

❏ Inventory your student safety gear. You must have goggles or other appropriate safety eyewear for each student in a class and a way to sanitize them at the end of each class, unless students have their own individual goggles. Other safety gear may be needed (e.g., aprons, gloves, tongs) depending on the activity.

❏ Check your room for compliance with ADA (Americans with Disabilities Act) requirements. For students who use wheelchairs, extra room may be needed and lab tables should be at the appropriate height. If students use assistive technologies for vision or hearing, determine if they can be used at your lab stations. Work with special education or guidance faculty to decide on the best way to accommodate student needs ahead of time so that they can participate as fully as possible in the class activities.

Decide how many students can work safely at each lab station. Most stations are set up for a maximum of four students. If you don't have enough lab stations for all students to work at once, you'll have to plan to work in shifts during the period or across several days, including seatwork for students who are waiting their turn. Students should never be unsupervised in the lab.

Your first activity should be one that does not require a lot of materials or have any hazards. During this dry run with full classes, circulate around the room. Remove anything that blocks student access to the lab stations or exits, such as extra desks, extension cords, or carts. Decide where students should stow their backpacks, coats, and other personal gear. Stand at each lab table to determine if students can see the board or screen. Look for any corners where you can't see the students.

The bottom line is that if your room is not equipped to do an activity safely, you can't do it, no matter how interesting or important you may think the activity is. Document the name of the activity and why it cannot be done safely. Although not as effective as the real experience, you can use alternatives (e.g., demonstrations, online simulations, video clips).

> As valuable as a lab might be to learning, there is no activity that is worth putting yourself or the students at risk.
>
> —Lisa, high school principal

Safety Contracts and Student Orientation

Sherrie

What should I include in a safety contract?

Find out if your science department has a standard "safety contract." This document alerts students and parents to safety issues and appropriate student behavior in the lab. This is not a legal document, but it can be an effective teaching tool for outlining student responsibilities. If your science department does not have a safety contract, a good place to start is NSTA's *Safety in the Science Classroom*, which provides a ready-to-use format complete with places for signatures. (→ See Resources and Online Appendix 5.1 for examples of contracts.)

Here are some examples of lab rules that would be common to any science course or grade level:

- Follow the teacher's directions. Do not attempt any procedure without the teacher's approval. Unsupervised lab work is not permitted.
- Notify the teacher immediately if anything is spilled or broken, if you or a lab partner is injured, or if equipment is not functioning properly.
- No equipment or materials are allowed to leave the lab without the teacher's permission.
- Food and drink are not permitted in the lab at any time. This includes lunch, snacks, or treats.
- Tasting materials used in the activity is not permitted.
- Running, pushing, practical jokes, or other horseplay is not permitted. Stay at your lab station unless it is your role to get equipment or materials.
- Dress appropriately for the lab. Long hair must be tied back. Loose or baggy clothing, dangling jewelry, and open-toe shoes or sandals are not appropriate.
- Protective eyewear (e.g., goggles) must be worn at all times when liquids, powders, heat, hammers, projectiles, or glassware are in use, both during the activity and during cleanup.
- Gloves or aprons may be required for some activities.
- Personal items (including electronics, purses, backpacks, or cosmetics) are not permitted at lab tables.
- Follow the teacher's directions for cleanup and disposal of any waste materials.

Add other requirements to the list, depending on your subject and the experience level of the students. For example, in a chemistry or physical science class, there should be rules for the safe handling of chemicals. For a biology or life science class, there should be rules for the safe handling of live and preserved specimens. Ask your department chair or safety officer about rules pertaining to contact lenses, especially in chemistry labs.

Hand out and discuss your safety contract. Explain that these rules are non-negotiable. Have each student sign a copy and put it in his or her notebook. Send two copies home—one to be returned with the signature of a parent or guardian and one to keep at home. Students should not be permitted to do an activity with potential hazards until you have a signed contract from both the student and parent. Summarize your safety guidelines in your course syllabus, on your website, and with the principal and safety officer.

Before your first activity, do an orientation with your classes. Don't assume they are aware of safety concerns. They may have had teachers who were relaxed in their use of safety procedures, or perhaps they have not had much lab experience. Review this orientation periodically and with new students:

- ❏ Locate the classroom exits.
- ❏ Demonstrate how and when to use safety equipment such as fire extinguishers or blankets.
- ❏ Know what to do in case of fire or chemical spills.
- ❏ Demonstrate how to turn off the water or gas.
- ❏ Locate materials needed for the activity, including goggles.

For fire drills and other emergencies, be sure you know which exits your student should use from the classroom and the building. Remind students on a regular basis, rather than waiting for the signal. Be sure to look out for students who may need assistance in responding to the alarm. Reinforce that students should leave in an orderly fashion. Find out what teachers need to do (e.g., turn off lights, close windows). Take a copy of your class list so that you can determine if everyone has left safely.

Lab Equipment and Supplies

As a science teacher, you have responsibilities for the storage, maintenance, and security of materials and equipment beyond those used in a regular classroom. If you inherited a lab and storage area that is potentially dangerous (e.g., unknown or mislabeled chemicals, spills, broken or rusty equipment, hazardous substances), it's your responsibility to enlist the support and assistance of your department chair and the safety officer in dealing with it. (→ See Online Appendix 5.2, "Chemical Safety.")

Storage

If you're short on space, items such as glassware or nonconsumable materials could be stored in lockable classroom cupboards or drawers. Label these areas with the contents. Chemicals or potentially hazardous materials, however, should never be stored in the classroom.

I teach my students that I have one word that I will say if there is an urgent need for them to pay attention due to a safety issue. That word is emergency! I never use it unless there is a true emergency and all students must stop what they are doing to pay attention to what they must do next. Other than times when the school emergency alarms have gone off, I have shouted "Emergency!" only twice in my career.

—Joclyn, grade 7 science teacher

For what types of materials am I required to have an MSDS on file?

Heather

For all chemicals you use, you must have Material Safety Data Sheets (MSDS) available and accessible. Most teachers have MSDS for acids, bases, solvents, and stains but are surprised they are necessary for common items you might purchase at a store (e.g., soap, cleaners, sodium bicarbonate, salt, glue, hand sanitizers). These sheets are issued by the manufacturers or suppliers and contain specific information about the substance: its composition, precautions for safe handling and use, potential hazards and interactions, health concerns, and disposal requirements. If you can't find the MSDS for the materials in your storage room, ask the safety officer. He or she should have a master collection for the school (see Resources at the end of this chapter).

All chemicals in the storage room must be labeled with date purchased and strength. Organize by type, not alphabetically by name. Store acids and bases separately. If you don't know what a chemical is, if it is dangerous (e.g., liquid mercury), or if it is not related to the curriculum, find out from the safety officer or the MSDS how to dispose of it. Never dispose of chemicals in the drain or trash can. (→ See Resources for safety-related information.)

The saying "a place for everything and everything in its place" is essential for a storage room. You'll want to be able to find things easily when you're planning an activity. Label the shelves, drawers, cupboards, and closets with what is found there. Small boxes are helpful for organizing and storing items. Photographs of what is behind a door or inside a drawer can be used to document where things are (or should be).

You may have been in high school or college biology labs full of jars with preserved specimens. They were interesting to look at, but the formaldehyde or formalin frequently used as a preservative at one time is a substance to be avoided today. According to the NSTA book *Investigating Safely,* "If you have formaldehyde or specimens preserved in formaldehyde from years ago, you cannot simply throw these materials away or dump the fluid down the sink. They are considered hazardous wastes and must be handled as such" (Texley, Kwan, and Summers 2004, p. 79). Specimens preserved in clear plastic blocks are safer for students to manipulate than those in jars of preservatives.

Security

By keeping chemicals and other lab materials and equipment in secure locations, you can minimize the chances of accidents or student mischief. Any materials or equipment you're not using on a given day should be in a locked location, and keys should be limited to you, other science teachers who need access, the safety officer, and the maintenance staff. Never share your key with another teacher, and don't give a key to a student to get something for you. In the lab, keep all drawers and cupboards locked, with the exception of those where you keep general

> Students should never be allowed in the storage area. In many situations the school insurance policy does not cover students in those areas.
>
> —Ty, middle school principal

classroom supplies. If the cupboards or drawers are not lockable, don't store any potentially hazardous materials or any specialized, valuable, or fragile equipment in them (e.g., balances, calculators, thermometers).

Ideally, your lab will have connected storage and prep rooms. Never allow students in these rooms. Don't use them for makeup labs or small-group work. Keep chemicals locked in a secure area within the storage room. If you share these rooms with an adjoining lab, be sure that the other teacher also keeps the doors locked at all times. You can never be too safe!

There are several benefits to having an up-to-date inventory in terms of both safety and security. Knowing what and how much you have and where it is stored is essential to keeping potentially hazardous materials out of the hands of others. Keep a copy of the inventory in the classroom and another in an off-site location (e.g., electronically on a network drive or a hard copy in the office).

Some of your equipment may have value outside of school and could be targeted by thieves. For valuable equipment (e.g., balances, laptops, electronic probes, calculators, projectors), record the serial numbers in your inventory and label with the school name (your maintenance staff may have tags or standard-ized ways of labeling). Keep these items locked up when not in use. If you notice something is missing, report it immediately to the principal.

Lab Activities

You'll be doing many types of activities in the lab: investigations, experiments, demonstrations, ongoing projects, and model building. Every activity should relate to your learning goals, be appropriate for the experience level of your students, and be conducted safely. There are many resources for finding lab activities—your textbook, curriculum guide, websites, and journal articles, to name a few. Although it's tempting to use them as is, you'll need to review them thoroughly to determine if you have the proper facilities and materials to conduct them safely. If you do not have access to a lab, your choice of activities is limited. (See Challenging Circumstances in this chapter.) Never have the students do an activity or procedure that you have not tried yourself.

- If your lab is not large enough to accommodate all of the students in a class, you can assign related seatwork to some of the students as they wait their turn. In cases such as this, the activity may take more than one class period.
- Prepare what students need in terms of materials and equipment. Avoid substituting materials unless you know they are equivalent. Have extras of materials so you don't have to leave the room to get something. As-semble trays or boxes with materials for each group. A card in the box (or notes on board) with an inventory helps students be accountable for returning items to their proper and safe locations.
- Prepare students for the activity by reviewing the procedures and safety precautions, even if you think the students know what to do. Put yourself

Be cautious of "gifts" of materials or equipment from well-meaning community members or parents. Check with your department chair on the school policy regarding these gifts. Politely decline anything that is inappropriate, unusable, or potentially hazardous.

—Richard, science department chair

Keep your eyes and ears open during a lab activity. Remain visible to all students, even if you're working with one group. I wear my lab coat so that students can locate me easily.

—Pat, grade 11 science teacher

in the role of a student. What could possibly go wrong? Approve any student-designed procedures before they start.

- Don't schedule an activity for a substitute, unless you know for sure the substitute is a credentialed science teacher and familiar with your lab and your routines. But even an experienced sub should not do activities that involve chemicals, flames, live specimens, projectiles, or heat sources. If in doubt, have an emergency packet available with seatwork or other safe activities. (→ See Chapter 4 for more on planning for a substitute.)

- Activities from older references may no longer be considered safe, such as those that involve body fluids (e.g., blood or saliva), live bacteria cultures, alcohol burners, or formaldehyde. Check with your safety officer for local and state regulations.

- Even your best class or your most advanced students can run into difficulties. Never leave the room or be distracted with e-mails or phone calls while students are doing an activity.

- Deal with incidents (such as spills or broken glass) immediately in a matter-of-fact manner. Then deal with the consequences of student horseplay or carelessness.

- Students doing seatwork should remain at their desks. If students get to class after the activity has started, allow them to work on the activity if and only if you brief them on the safety issues (as you did with the rest of the class at the beginning of the activity).

Some of my students grumble when I make them wear eye protection. "Mr. X never made us do this." How should I respond?

Alberto

If a student is engaging in potentially dangerous behavior and does not respond to your guidelines, remove the student from the situation immediately, stopping the entire class if necessary. You may have students complain about your rules concerning eyewear or other safety precautions, saying that other teachers do not have such rules. Your response is firm: I am concerned about your health and safety. Model the appropriate behavior by following your own rules concerning eyewear and attire. (→ See Online Appendix 5.3, "Safety Goggles for Your Laboratory.")

It seems like I run out of time on lab days. What can I do to streamline the end of the period?

Tanya

Time flies during an activity, and if the bell rings while students are still working, they'll want to rush on to their next class. Students must assume responsibility for cleaning up at the end of the period so everything is secured safely and ready for the next class.

- Assign one student from the group as the safety supervisor to make sure the group members complete tasks such as returning the materials to the proper places, wiping the tabletop, cleaning the glassware, turning off or resetting probes and other instruments, discarding any trash in the proper receptacle, following other directions you may have (such as sterilizing and storing eyewear), and washing their hands.
- Check each group's lab station and their box or tray to inventory the equipment and materials. The contents of the tray or box should match the list in the box or on the board. Do not dismiss the class until the cleanup is complete and you have checked that all materials are accounted for.
- At the end of the day, secure all materials and equipment. If you're continuing an activity, put the boxes in the storage room. If the activity is completed, put things in their proper place. Don't put anything away that is dirty or broken.

> I become very involved during class as I have so many things that require my attention. To prevent not being ready for the end of class, I have an official "time keeper" to give me a five-minute warning!
> —Dwayne, grade 9 science teacher

Challenging Circumstances

> *Some of my classes meet in a regular classroom. Can I safely do labs there?*
>
> Jason

The ideal situation is one science teacher per laboratory, but with enrollment and space issues this is not always the case. In some schools, teachers with low seniority may be assigned to teach science in a regular classroom or travel from room to room for their classes.

A regular classroom does not have running water, ventilation, and safety equipment (such as goggles, an eyewash station, or a fire blanket). There may be slanted desks instead of flat tables. Accept the fact that there will be many hands-on activities you cannot do safely in a regular classroom, despite the curriculum or student interest. These classrooms are probably not connected to science storage rooms and may not have lockable storage, so you will have to plan for safely moving the equipment and materials that you are able to use. Regulations may specify that you may not move some items through hallways used by students. Check with your department chair or safety officer concerning these restrictions before moving items.

If you're a "floater" (a teacher who moves from room to room throughout the day), you'll face additional obstacles. You are in the hallways at the same time as the students, so transporting materials and equipment can be hazardous. You'll arrive at and leave the room at the same time as the students, so planning and

> When I was a floater in another building, I made sure that I had a lockable cabinet in each room to keep things safe.
>
> —Richard, science department chair

organization are important to save valuable class time. At the very least, you should be given a lockable cart and an elevator key.

In these situations, you will be limited in what you can do beyond paper-and-pencil assignments, discussions, or simple activities that do not require a lot of materials or equipment. Be sure to document which activities you are unable to do, in case anyone questions your decision. You can use videos and technology-based simulations to provide experiences for the students.

Sharing a lab with a nonscience class is a potentially dangerous situation. Although it's an inconvenience, before you leave the classroom, all equipment and materials must be secured, the gas and water must be turned off, and doors to the storage and prep rooms must be locked. Share your safety guidelines, especially those concerning food in the lab or the use of the lab refrigerator.

Sharing a lab with another science teacher is not as much of an issue, but it's not an ideal situation for either of you. Have a set of mutually agreed-upon safety guidelines and contracts and procedures for inventories. Develop a schedule for lab days, so that both of you are not trying to set up activities on the same day. As a courtesy, divide up teacher desk space and bulletin board space and have a common area for general class supplies. If your "roommate" violates any safety regulations or engages in hazardous activities, document the incident and share it with an administrator, the safety officer, and your department chair.

A class period interrupted by lunch is especially challenging for science instruction. Your activities have to be designed to start and stop, and you'll have double the transition times (going to and returning from lunch). Ask your principal if some days you can have an uninterrupted period, mentioning safety issues that may arise from stopping and starting lab activities or leaving the room in the middle of the activity.

Conclusion

It is a challenge to engage students in planned and purposeful science investigations that are also interesting and relevant to them. Safety concerns can seem overwhelming, but knowledge of the issues, planning (and overplanning), awareness, and common sense will see you through.

Resources *(www.nsta.org/riseandshine)*

NSTA Books

Kwan, T., and J. Texley. 2002. *Exploring safely: A guide for elementary teachers.* Arlington, VA: NSTA Press.

Kwan, T., and J. Texley. 2003. *Inquiring safely: A guide for middle school teachers.* Arlington, VA: NSTA Press.

Roy, K. 2007. *The NSTA ready-reference guide to safer science: An NSTA Press journals collection.* Arlington, VA: NSTA Press.

Texley, J., T. Kwan, and J. Summers. 2004. *Investigating safely: A guide for high school teachers.* Arlington, VA: NSTA Press.

Websites About Plants and Animals in the Classroom

Common Houseplants Poisonous to People and Pets: *www.denverplants.com/foliage/ html/Poisonous_Plants.htm*

Common Poisonous Plants and Plant Parts: *http://aggie-horticulture.tamu.edu/ lawn_garden/poison/poison.html*

NSTA Position Statement: Responsible Use of Live Animals and Dissection in the Science Classroom: *www.nsta.org/about/positions/animals.aspx*

Principles and Guidelines for the Use of Animals in Precollege Education: *www.nabt. org/websites/institution/File/Principles%20and%20Guidelines%20for%20the%20 Use%20of%20Animals%20in%20Precollege%20Education.pdf*

Safe and Poisonous Houseplants: *www.ladybug.uconn.edu/hotissues/ SafeandPoisonousHouseplants.html*

Toxicity of Common Houseplants: *http://lancaster.unl.edu/factsheets/031.htm*

Use of Animals in Biology Education: *www.nabt.org/websites/institution/index. php?p=97*

Websites About Safety Issues and Safety Contracts

General Lab Safety Recommendation (from CSSS): *www.csss-science.org/ recommendations.shtml*

General Science Safety Checklist (from CSSS): *www.csss-science.org/checklist.shtml*

Laboratory Safety Guidelines: 40 Suggestions for a Safer Lab (from ICASE): *www. icaseonline.net/lsi.pdf*

NSTA Position Statement: Liability of Science Educators for Laboratory Safety: *www.nsta.org/about/positions/liability.aspx*

NSTA Safety Portal: *www.nsta.org/portals/safety.aspx*

Safe Science Series (NSELA): *www.nsela.org/index.php?option=com_content&view =category&id=71&Itemid=79*

Safety Resources: Red Clay, SD: *http://rccsecondaryscience.wikispaces.com/ Safety+Resources*

Safety in the Science Classroom (Safety Contract): *www.nsta.org/pdfs/ SafetyInTheScienceClassroom.pdf*

School Laboratory Safety Courses (free online courses from Flinn Scientific): *http:// labsafety.flinnsci.com/Home.aspx*

Science & Safety: Making the Connection (a secondary safety guide from CSSS): *www.csss-science.org/downloads/scisafe.pdf*

Science Education Safety (from CSSS): *www.csss-science.org/safety.shtml*

Science and Safety: It's Elementary (an elementary safety guide from CSSS): *www. csss-science.org/downloads/scisaf_cal.pdf*

SIRI MSDS Index: *http://siri.org/msds*

Student safety contracts and exams (from Flinn Scientific): *http://www.flinnsci.com/ teacher-resources/safety/safety-contracts-and-safety-exams*

SciLinks

Chemical Handling and Safety: *www.scilinks.org/fromoutside.asp?type=teacher&sci LINKSNumber=slmk117*

Chemical Safety: *www.scilinks.org/fromoutside.asp?type=teacher&sciLINKSNumber =slm9365*

Laboratory Safety: *www.scilinks.org/fromoutside.asp?type=teacher&sciLINKSNumber =slm5629*

Safety in the Science Classroom: *www.scilinks.org/fromoutside.asp?type=teacher& sciLINKSNumber=slm91404*

Online Appendixes

5.1 NSTA Safety Agreement

5.2 Chemical Safety

5.3 Safety Goggles for Your Laboratory

CHAPTER 6
YOUR ATTITUDE MATTERS

Sherrie

Dear Ms. Mentor,

We learned several strategies for writing in science classes during our last inservice. But when I tried one in my classroom, it went over like a lead balloon. What was I doing wrong?

Dear Sherrie,

How many times have we heard "Well, I tried [fill in the blank], but it didn't work"? And then the classroom instruction reverts to the tried and (not necessarily) true methods. This certainly happened to me when I tried a different instructional strategy, an alternative form of assessment, or a new classroom management routine. Students would roll their eyes or complain before we even started.

I've come to the conclusion that any type of change is difficult for some people (not an original thought on my part). We are such creatures of habit! By the time students are in the upper elementary grades, they have a definite attitude about what school is "supposed to be." Whenever teachers or administrators deviate from this comfort zone, the defenses go up.

Students are not the only ones whose attitudes are based on their comfort zones. Just try a different format for a faculty meeting, a new schedule for inservice days, or a strategy to get teachers out of their seats at a workshop. I had a graduate student in one of my classes who was incredulous that I expected them to work cooperatively and to participate in class discussions. "I didn't know we were going to have to, like, do anything!" she remarked with an angry look. I had obviously encroached on her comfort zone.

I'm not sure who invented the three-time rule, but the rule seems true: Once is an event and twice is a coincidence, but after the third time a trend or pattern is established. If we try a new strategy once and it doesn't fit the status quo, the students may assume that if they fuss or refuse, we'll say, "Well, that didn't work," and classroom life will return to the way things are supposed to be.

But if we know that something is research based or that it will ultimately pay off in better learning or an improved classroom environment, we should stick with the plan and explain why we are doing something new or different. We may need to model the new activity or procedure too.

This actually turned into several action research projects for me. As I was implementing something new, I noted what the responses were and by whom. I reflected on whether I was implementing the new strategy appropriately and how I had introduced it. After all, my students weren't any different from others. Why would something work in many other classrooms across the country but not in mine?

Being aware of the three-time rule (event, coincidence, pattern) and understanding that it often takes several attempts before attitudes change—whether by students or teachers—worked for me. Just give yourself some time and keep at it. You will develop the confidence and become more positive. If it's the right thing to do, students will internalize it, and soon what was once a new idea becomes part of the way things are supposed to be.

—Ms. Mentor

WHEN YOU SEE a purpose in what you do, feel confident, and like what you do, it shows. Students are among those who can immediately read others. They will know if you are eager to get to school each day, if you enjoy what you teach, and if you care and are sincere in wanting to support them as they try to do their best. Teachers who feel good about themselves, their students, and their school are more likely to reach out to students and support their learning, make them feel better about themselves, and create a dynamic learning environment.

Qualities of an Effective Teacher

 What are some of the attributes that are considered to be critical in being an effective teacher?

Tanya

There are many lists available that identify the qualities of a good teacher. The following qualities have been selected from several of those lists (Colker 2010; Haskvitz 2002):

- *Collegiality:* You are not in this alone. One of the first things you should do to create a positive attitude is link up with others in your building. Find positive people with whom you can share, laugh, and confide. You will find the mutual support you can give one another will go a long way in helping you keep spirits high. A collegial relationship can also add greatly to you professionally. You can be a more effective teacher by developing connections with your peers. You can begin this by pairing up with another beginning teacher or getting involved in online communities of teachers. (→ See Chapter 11, "Finding Support.")

- *Positive expectations:* Knowing what you and your students can or cannot achieve is an expectation. You predispose yourself to positive outcomes when you have set them as expectations. Set high expectations and let your students (and parents) know you have set this bar. Many people say that it takes just as much energy to achieve positive results as negative results.

- *Classroom management:* Learning to manage your class instead of disciplining your class should be a priority. This means you should immediately find ways to have a highly organized, well-managed classroom where students can learn. Management refers to everything you do to organize the space, materials, equipment, time, students, and instruction. That includes layout, cleanliness, organization, displays, accessibility and availability of lab equipment, materials, and progression of learning. It is key to have everything ready for students before they walk in the door. Let them see that you are prepared for them (→ see Chapter 4 for more on classroom management).

- *Flexibility:* Even the most deliberately well-planned lesson can go wrong. That is part of what happens in science. Turn the potential disasters into teachable moments that can provide learning opportunities for your students. You must be flexible and take advantage of every teachable moment. Overplan and have a backup plan as another activity you might include if the current lesson is failing.

- *Empathy:* Consider what is happening in the lives of your students. If there is a huge pep rally and the big game is Saturday, then consider whether Monday is the best day to have a long-term assignment due. The ultimate application of this skill is knowing of problems that individual students may face and then helping them do their best given the situation.

- *Patience:* Sometimes it is difficult to remember that students are learners. If they had already developed a conceptual understanding of the science topic they are studying, then they wouldn't need you to teach it to them. Be patient with them. Slice back on a topic if it requires more scaffolding, chunk out the concepts in manageable pieces, give students more time to learn and understand, or repeat difficult information in different ways to meet their needs. Learning is not a race.

- *Mastery of teaching science:* It's said that if the student has failed to learn, we have failed the student. Developing mastery in the field of science and in the pedagogy of instruction is essential to being an effective teacher. Your learning did not end when you left the university. As a matter of fact, it has only begun. You will find that there are many more science concepts and teaching strategies to learn. Teachers are lifelong learners ($\rightarrow$ see Chapter 9, "Creating Professional Development Opportunities").

Effective teachers provide the opportunities for students to be effective learners. But another one of the benefits of being an effective teacher is that you will have fewer discipline problems. Students will know what to do, how to follow routines and procedures, and what your expectations are for them ($\rightarrow$ see Chapter 4, "Creating an Environment for Learning").

Some Other Qualities to Keep in Mind

Supporting the Team

Teaching teams and the science department make the workload easier, the task more pleasant, and the outcomes potentially more valuable. There are specific steps you can take to become a valuable member of a team. Consider this list of important parts of supporting the team. Reflect and compare it to your behaviors.

> Remember that students don't care what you know until they know you care.
>
> —Dale, grade 3 teacher

- ❏ Listen to the opinions of others before you make decisions. Listen more than you talk.
- ❏ Value the experience of others.
- ❏ Work toward the goals determined by the team.
- ❏ Be understanding and supportive.
- ❏ Be on time for everything.
- ❏ Do your share. Show your willingness to carry part of the load.
- ❏ When you make a commitment, keep your promise.
- ❏ Treat everyone in the school community with courtesy.
- ❏ Celebrate the hard work and contributions of others.
- ❏ Admit when you are not sure of something.
- ❏ Be a cheerleader for your team and the school.
- ❏ Do not gossip.
- ❏ Conduct yourself in a professional manner.
- ❏ Show your willingness to continue to improve.

Creativity

Step outside the box. Find new and interesting ways to teach topics. Being creative will not only keep your students actively engaged but also provide you with newfound interest in topics you may not have considered interesting in the past.

> They may forget what you said. They'll always remember how you made them feel.
>
> —Shayna, special education teacher

You need to develop new ways of looking at science content and instructional strategies. You will find it necessary to reteach or reinforce concepts in a variety of ways. Being able to look at the material in a new way and then sharing that with students who may struggle with the concept is important. One way to develop this sense is by looking at the way other teachers handle the same science concept. Consider how they creatively teach the concept and related skills. Perhaps it is a matter of changing the sequence—maybe some lectures become labs or the textbook might be replaced with articles from periodicals or web-based reading. Consider the variety of approaches that might be used to teach the same concept and skills in different ways. (→ See Chapter 7 for more on differentiation.)

Exhibiting a Sense of Humor

No one wants to enter a classroom where there is a grouchy person in control. Smile at your students, even if you don't feel like smiling. It is likely that they are not the reason for your lack of a smile. Let them know you are happy to see them.

Find novel ways to interject humor in your lessons. Check websites for cartoons, funny sayings, or illustrations that apply to the science concept you are teaching. Post it on your whiteboard or overhead projector.

Something is bound to go wrong in a science investigation or a demonstration you are conducting. Instead of attempting to cover it up or deny it, let yourself and the class laugh at it. It might prove to be a wonderful teachable moment. Provide an upbeat atmosphere. Science class doesn't need to be all laughs, but it should be joyous. Play music that fits the science concept you are teaching, tell anecdotal stories surrounding the concept, wear a costume, stage a re-enactment, say something outrageous for students to react to, play a silly game to help them remember the steps in a procedure, or have "celebrations" for the birth of a famous scientist or anniversary of a discovery. But when having fun, do not use sarcasm. Although it may be funny to some students, others may be hurt by it.

Amnesia

Forget about it. Holding a grudge or bringing up past errors is an unhealthy way to develop relationships and move forward. That is true in your personal life, and it is true in the classroom. Forget about the discipline errors your students may have made in the past. Treat them with respect and let them know you anticipate they will follow regulations and move on. Of course, if they repeat the error frequently, you can't forget about it. That will only lead to the loss of control of not only that student but others as well. You must also continue to be aware of and deal with students who behave unsafely in the science lab.

Self-Care: Your Physical and Mental Health

We probably should have put this section first in the book and then repeated it for you frequently. New teachers believe they can do it all. It's an eagerness to be supportive of student learning (at the expense of everything else) that pushes teachers into the time drain. What monopolizes your time both in class and during times you plan to use for class preparation? If you recognize the problems, you can do something about it. Think of ways to streamline tasks, prioritize, and emphasize those tasks that warrant that extra effort (Fredericks 2005):

- Classroom discipline
- Taking attendance and other noninstructional activities
- Visitors

> Three days I celebrate every year are Pi Day (March 14), Mole Day (October 23 and June 2), and GIS Day (November 17).
>
> —Dwayne, grade 9 science teacher

- Noises, distractions, and unplanned interruptions (emergency drills, assemblies, announcements)
- Distributing and collecting papers
- Conferencing and telephone calls
- Paperwork and clerical tasks
- Bus, hall, and cafeteria duty
- Grading and record keeping
- Extras: coaching athletic or academic teams, coming in early to set up lessons, cleaning up the labs, inventorying equipment and supplies, and spending holidays and vacations doing research or looking for new teaching ideas

No wonder teachers are worn out at the end of the day. According to a Health magazine study (reported in Tolison 2008), the most stressful job in the United States is that of an inner-city high school teacher. Other sources place firefighters, police officers, air traffic controllers, surgeons and the president of the United States in that category too (Brienza 2011; Rivers 2010; Tracey 2010). That should give you pretty good idea as to the stress level we are talking about. The average classroom teacher makes more than 1,500 educational decisions every school day, which averages out to more than 4 decisions every minute (Fredericks 2005). Air traffic control specialists are considered members of a profession that must make the most decisions per hour of any profession (D'Arcy and Della Rocco 2001). They are in a dynamic environment involving many actors, constant updating of relevant information, and, sometimes conflicting goals. They often need to make difficult decisions with incomplete information, under time pressure, and with a large workload—sound familiar?

Attempting to do it all can cause nothing but burnout. Here are some ways to prevent burnout before it hits you:

- ❑ Listen to your body. Admit stress and pressure.
- ❑ Don't do everything alone. Participate in activities with others both at school and in your social life.
- ❑ As tempting as it is to save time and eat at your desk—don't. Eating food in the lab is not a good idea, so eat in an appropriate location with others every day and talk about something other than school.
- ❑ Re-assess what is important. Do you need to do everything in the same way you have previously?
- ❑ Considering that you only have so much energy, what is worth your energy? Pace yourself.
- ❑ Take care of your body. Eat well, get plenty of sleep, keep a disinfectant handy and use it, keep your hands away from your face, exercise, go to the doctor for checkups, and stay at home when ill.
- ❑ Diminish worry and anxiety. Five steps to take to diminish this stress include being physically active, eating healthy food, avoiding overuse of alcohol or other drugs, practicing relaxation exercise, and taking time for yourself.
- ❑ Learn to say no.

> When I begin to feel stressed, I walk away from it for a while. There are several things I enjoy doing, like yard work. A little of that usually brings me to a point that I can go back and deal with the stress.
>
> —Sharon, grade 5 teacher

Time is one of the greatest enemies of science teachers. Most science teachers have a more intense workload than other teachers in the building. You are setting up and cleaning up labs, managing materials for students, and being constantly diligent in monitoring safety in your classroom. As teachers, we get involved in too many tasks that are outside our classroom responsibilities: We volunteer for too many projects, say yes to too many committees, or take on duties simply because somebody asked us. Teachers tend to be tireless in what they are willing to do for their students and the school. And the more you do, the more you will be asked to do. What's the solution? Take control of your time by planning realistically and start by saying no. ($\rightarrow$ See Online Appendix 6.1 for suggestions to prevent burnout.)

> *I've been asked to coach the engineering team but I simply feel I don't have time. Can I say no?*
>
> Jason

As a new teacher, you must select out-of-classroom and beyond-the-school-day activities wisely. If you handle these activities well, people will respect you more for saying no rather than saying yes and finding yourself without the time and resources necessary to do your job well. Consider these ways to say no:

- I'd really like to, but I am involved in providing the best experiences for my classes on [current topic] and it is requiring a lot of my time right now.
- I'm so pleased that you have confidence in my abilities. I hope you will ask me again at some time in the future because I'm just too busy to take this on right now.
- Thanks for asking, but I really need to spend some more quality time with my [children, spouse, friends] and I can't do that and also provide the amount of time I need to dedicate to my classes this first year.
- No, thank you. I'm not ready to take on that additional responsibility just yet. I hope I can participate next year when I've had a little more experience.

You can save time on repetitive tasks by initiating some of these easy-to-implement strategies:

- Assign some of the everyday tasks to students. You will benefit and so will your students as they take on these classroom responsibilities:
  - Appoint someone to take attendance.
  - Assign a student to answer the door and welcome visitors to the classroom. Since most visitors are there to deliver information, this frees you to continue with a lesson.
  - Assign a materials person. Label all of your materials bins and cabinets. Give one or more students lists of items you need for the

> I come into school early each day. The quiet of the building and my classroom is a peaceful and gentle way to start. My head is clear and I can prepare for the students. It's like the calm before the storm.
>
> —Dale, grade 3 teacher

day and have them pull them from the bins. The same students can be responsible for putting materials back in their designated space the next morning as other students pull the materials for that day. This is a great activity for students in your homeroom or those who like to hang around after school. Just a word of caution that you should be certain all materials students will handle are safe. The storage room should be off-limits.

- Constantly be on the lookout for ways to engage your students in classroom tasks.

- Writing classroom passes take time. Create a pass template and make several copies. Have students fill out their own pass and you simply provide initials. Or, instead of using paper passes for students to leave and use the restroom, make a pass that can be worn on a chain around a student's neck so the pass can be used repeatedly.

- Instead of collecting papers from each student, have them hand materials in baskets labeled with the following:
  - Get yesterday's homework assignment from here.
  - Get today's homework assignment from here.
  - Completed homework
  - Incomplete homework
  - Late homework

Science teachers often grossly underestimate the amount of time outside school they will need to spend on planning and setting up labs, cleaning and maintaining lab equipment, gathering needed materials and equipment, grading papers, evaluating, communicating with parents, and providing feedback to students. New teachers too often neglect their health and families as they attempt to do everything. To be effective over the long term for students, accomplished teachers learn to balance their lives. If you need more support in this area, refer to the article "Well-Balanced Teacher: How to Work Smarter and Stay Sane Inside the Classroom and Out" (Anderson 2010; → see Resources).

Alberto

I assigned too much homework. I now have mountains of papers and no time to get them graded and back to students to make the learning valuable. What can I do with these assignments?

One way to cut down on the time required to conduct high-quality, effective lab experiences is to structure the requirements you make of your students in such a way that they will not require as much of your time for grading. First, carefully decide the importance of components of assignments and which components must be assessed and graded. If you have a stack of papers, don't feel you must grade every student entry. Decide if it's necessary to return every assignment the following day. Perhaps the most important factor to focus on in a given assignment is the data analysis, or perhaps it is the strategies they used to control variables. Grade and comment on only that portion. Be sure students know that this is what you have done. This way they will not believe the entire paper has been assessed. (→ See Online Appendix 6.2 for more tips for cutting down on time needed for assessing student work, as well as Chapter 8, "Assessment Literacy.")

Passion for Your Subject and Your Students

I have read some research as to the qualities of exceptional teachers. But, what do students consider to be important characteristics of a good teacher?

Heather

You have selected this profession because you enjoy teaching science. Now you need to let the students know it. You should show that you care about your students and their success in learning. It's important that students feel they are important to you. With so many demands on your time, this may be difficult to keep in the foreground of your efforts. To get to know students better, take advantage of the moments before class begins, the times you pass students in the halls, or the few minutes at the end of class as students pack up their belongings. It's also possible to find time to speak with them as they are gathering data in an investigation or setting up an apparatus. Do not be afraid to let them know you care about what they think and feel.

Sincerity and respect can be shown in many ways, and you cannot underestimate how each of your actions affects how students will interpret actions. You should act in a mature manner at all times. Even though you and your students should have fun in class, there are boundaries. You are the adult and should behave in an adult manner. Here's a list of things you should *not* do:

- Make comments that are playful insults (no sarcasm)
- Lose your temper
- Be untruthful
- Ignore students
- Play favorites
- Use inappropriate language or gestures

Knowing your subject matter is important in showing that you enjoy science; it allows you to respond to students' interests that might be at a greater depth than your planned lessons. It also indicates to them the energy you have given to the pursuit of your interest in the subject matter. Get excited along with the students when they make new discoveries and connect concepts to new understanding.

The following list is taken from a variety of sources and indicates what students want from teachers in the classroom (ASCD 2008; Carlson 2009; Raynaud n.d.; Smyth 2011; Wasserman 2010):

- Explains material well and provides opportunities to learn
- Listens to all students
- Enjoys being in the classroom
- Knows a lot about science and enjoys teaching it
- Respects students
- Helps students learn
- Doesn't ever embarrass the student
- Doesn't give too much homework or busy work
- Treats everyone fairly
- Returns papers promptly
- Makes learning fun
- Not too strict but not a pushover
- Makes the student feel comfortable in the classroom

Conclusion

If you wonder how much your attitude matters, simply think back to the teachers who stand out in your mind as being exceptional. You may want to look at the lists above and compare your recollections with these traits. What you probably didn't know is that they more than likely felt the same type of stress you are experiencing as you enter the profession. They undoubtedly had strategies similar to the ones you will need for coping with this stress.

Resources *(www.nsta.org/riseandshine)*

Anderson, M. 2010. *Well-balanced teacher: How to work smarter and stay sane inside the classroom and out.* Reston, VA: Association for Supervision and Curriculum Development.

Gloetzer, T. 2008. Anxiety treatment—5 effective strategies to decrease anxiety. *http://ezinearticles.com/?Anxiety-Treatment---5-Effective-Strategies-to-Decrease-Anxiety&id=1198780*

National Education Association (NEA). 2010. Mental Health and Wellness. *www.neahin.org/health-safety/mental.* The National Education Association (NEA) website offers support in several areas, including suggestions for managing stress and anxiety. The site identifies causes and steps to take to overcome the situations.

Rosales, J. 2011. Surviving teacher burnout. *NEA Today.* National Education Association. *http://neatoday.org/2011/06/07/surviving-teacher-burnout*

Online Appendixes

6.1. Checklist for Burnout Prevention

6.2. Tips for Cutting Down on Time Needed for Student Work Assessment

CHAPTER 7
TEACHING STRATEGIES

Tanya

Dear Ms. Mentor,

My ninth-grade students enjoy labs, but my colleagues say I do too many and the students aren't learning anything. How many labs should I do each week?

Dear Tanya,

Some teachers use the word *lab* to describe a variety of activities, from investigations and experiments to cookbook demonstrations, small-group discussions, simulations, group writing assignments, and laptop activities—anything students do in groups in science class. While all of these activities can be part of useful learning strategies, let's assume you are referring to inquiry-based investigations.

NSTA's position on scientific inquiry states, "Scientific inquiry is a powerful way of understanding science content. Students learn how to ask questions and use evidence to answer them. In the process of learning the strategies of scientific inquiry, students learn to conduct an investigation and collect evidence from a variety of sources, develop an explanation from the data, and communicate and defend their conclusions" (NSTA 2004).

Although you don't have to justify your choice of learning activities (or their frequency) to your colleagues, you can reflect on them for your own professional peace of mind. As you design activities, it may be helpful to parse NSTA's position statement.

Ask whether your labs help students do the following:

- Understand science content—the processes and "big ideas" as well as facts and concepts
- Ask questions (not just answer ones that someone else asks)
- Design and conduct investigations related to the questions
- Collect and organize evidence (data)
- Analyze evidence to develop an explanation
- Communicate and defend their conclusions

This is a lot to expect of students. They'll need guidance and modeling tailored to their level of experience. I observed Joclyn, who scaffolded the inquiry process for her students. She kept the unit's "big idea" posted in the classroom and referred to it during every activity (lab or otherwise) to keep the students focused on the learning goals. When she asked students for questions to investigate, she added a few of her own as a model. She guided the students through a discussion of how the experiment was designed and how the design related to the question. (After experiencing various types of investigations, they took over more of the design process.) She monitored the students as they conducted the investigation (assisting and intervening when necessary) and collected data. She worked with the students as they reviewed their data and discussed how the data did or did not relate to the question. The teacher recognized this was a time-consuming process, but she was confident they were learning (and the assessment results supported this conclusion).

There really isn't a numeric answer to your question. For scientific inquiry the quality of the activities is more important than the quantity. Doing an activity for the sake of doing an activity without any follow-up or reflection may lead to the second concern about what the students actually learn from the activity and whether they truly understand the concepts or the inquiry process.

—Ms. Mentor

AFTER MANY YEARS of teaching and reflecting, you will have a collection of successful strategies to use with your class. This will become your own personal repertoire to use in situations you face every day. During your years of trying various strategies, you will find that some work fabulously for you in many situations while others are more focused and work better in limited situations. Don't expect all teaching strategies to work for you every time. If a strategy doesn't seem to work, reflect on possible reasons. But don't be afraid to try new ways to reach students and support them in learning science.

Motivating Your Class

Think about your own learning experiences. In what situations were you the most eager to learn? Was it in a class where the teacher enthusiastically dove into each experience, or was it a class when the teacher introduced you to new information in a dour manner? Your students will react to the way you communicate with them. If you think highly of them and encourage them, they will respond. You are the most significant motivating factor in your classroom.

What can I do to motivate my class and keep everyone engaged?

Sherrie

As a teacher, you can threaten, cajole, plead, or reward students into doing what you want, but the ultimate decision about how much to participate is made by the students. Here are some ways to create lessons that will help you motivate students:

- *Make it real:* To foster intrinsic motivation, try to create learning activities based on topics that are relevant to your students. This is easy to do in science with topics such as DNA and heredity, forensics, simple machines, weather and climate, and environmental issues. Some students see these connections immediately; others may need guidance and examples. Use local examples, events in the news, and technology (iPods, cell phones, video clips), and take advantage of teachable moments that connect the subject with your students' real-life interests, concerns, hobbies, and backgrounds.
- *Provide audiences for student work:* When students know their work will be placed on display, published, read out loud, or shared with parents, they may take it more seriously and will likely give it their all.
- *Create appropriate rigor:* Students perform best when the level of difficulty is slightly above their current ability level. If the task is too easy, it promotes boredom and may communicate a sense that the teacher believes the students are not capable of better work. A task that is too difficult may feel unattainable and create anxiety or a sense of defeat.
- *Use projects and open-ended questions:* These assignments give students an opportunity to use their higher-level thinking skills and creativity. Open-ended questions also eliminate some of the risk of failure students may feel.
- *Celebrate successes:* Give frequent, early, and positive feedback that supports students' beliefs that they can do well. Students can also learn by watching a peer succeed at a task. (→ See Chapter 8 for more on providing informative feedback.)

Share your own interests, experience, or passion for the topic. Even if the topic is not of great interest to you personally, you never know what will spark something in a student. So at least pretend to be interested in the topic. If you say, "This next unit is pretty dull, but we have to cover it for the test," you're not setting the stage to engage students.

—Sharon, grade 5 teacher

> I have found that just saying "I want you to do your best" doesn't provide results. It's important to be more specific with concrete directions as to what their "best" looks like. Mentioning something they did exceptionally well in the past as a touchstone or asking that they improve on a specific aspect helps.
>
> —Joclyn, grade 7 science teacher

- *Establish a sense of belonging:* People have a fundamental need to feel connected or related to other people. In an academic environment, research shows that students who feel they belong have a higher degree of intrinsic motivation and academic confidence (Goodenow 1992; Marzano, Pickering, and Heflebower 2010; Wilms 2000). Students say their sense of belonging is fostered by a teacher who demonstrates warmth and openness; encourages student participation; is enthusiastic, friendly, and helpful; and is organized and prepared for class. Use students' names in examples and questions. Support a feeling that students are valued members of a learning community. You can accomplish this by listening, giving hints and encouragement, being responsive to student questions, and showing empathy for students. (→ See Chapter 3 for more on motivating students.)

- *Provide choices:* Students can have increased motivation when they feel some sense of their role in constructing their experiences. Allow students to occasionally pick their own lab partners or select from alternate assignments. Full-inquiry investigations provide a feeling of empowerment because students are given many opportunities for making choices as they complete the investigation. More complex ways to involve them is through "contract learning," where students can determine their own due dates, assignments, or products. They determine how they will learn and may even select what they will learn. The more formal name for this method is independent study, but you can provide this in a less formal manner (see "Differentiation," p. 78).

- *Ask students to evaluate themselves:* When students know they will have input in the evaluation of their work, they are more likely to work toward the goals. This input is supported through providing students with a rubric that establishes accountability.

- *Strategize with struggling students:* Identify the learning problems students face. Be specific in addressing their needs and communicate your belief in their abilities. Then go on to support them in their learning.

- *Arouse students' curiosity:* This can be done through provocative questioning or by providing intriguing examples, such as a discrepant event. A discrepant event puzzles observers; it is contrary to what students expect (a discrepancy in understanding), causing them to wonder about what is occurring. With proper guidance from you, students will attempt to figure out the discrepancy and begin the process of seeking an explanation for the situation. This might be a connection to previous learning or may initiate a new question or inquiry. A quick internet search will provide you with many examples of discrepant events (see the resources list at the end of this chapter).

Once the motivation momentum is established, step back and see how much students can accomplish. But don't rely on infrequent motivational tools to keep them going. You must be diligent about this strategy and make it a part of what you do each day. Keep motivation in mind as you plan.

Modeling

In working with students, you can't assume anything. For example, you might ask them to brainstorm, reflect, read and take notes, or review for a test, but they may not really know how to do these. They could exhibit their frustration through disruptive behaviors, adding to their problems. Model the processes you want them to use through "think alouds," in which you literally talk your way through a process, making the process visible (and audible). Make some intentional mistakes, verbalize how you recognize the errors, and ask the students how you could deal with the errors.

What should I do? I asked my students to brainstorm with the group. I provided a definition of brainstorming but no one seemed to know how to go about it.

— Heather

Show the students what a well-written lab report, project, data summary, response to a test question, diagram, or science notebook looks like—they may have never seen one before. Take notes together at first to show students how to find and record important information. Break down a task into small, doable components that lead to a successful finished product. Plan for most assignments to be completed in class at first so you can guide the students through the task. After a while, these "scaffolds" can (and should) be scaled down for most students; other students may need continued support.

The basic guideline here is to consider what you want your students to provide and then give them an example. Don't just tell them what is expected—show them.

Overcoming Misconceptions

How do I know if students have a clear understanding of the background necessary to deal with the concepts they will be learning in my class?

— Alberto

Misconceptions are also referred to as alternate ideas, nonscientific beliefs, naive theories, preconceived notions, or conceptual misunderstandings. Basically, in science these are situations in which something a person knows and believes is inaccurate or scientifically incorrect. Most people (students and adults) who hold misconceptions are not aware that their ideas are incorrect. When a person is told that their ideas are not correct, they often have a hard time giving up their misconceptions—especially if they have held a misconception for a long time.

Possessing misconceptions can have a serious effect on our learning. Students continue to build knowledge on their current understandings, whether those understandings are correct or not. There are several steps you can take toward eliminating student misconceptions in science:

❏ Learn common misconceptions. The best way to help students overcome misconceptions is by increasing your knowledge about them and identifying them. Begin by becoming familiar with some of the most commonly held misconceptions. You can find these on the web by searching for misconceptions in the specific content area under study. Once you have an understanding of these misconceptions, you will be able to spot them easily when they become evident in your class. A few examples are listed below:
- o Insects are not animals.
- o Sound can be heard in outer space.
- o Fertilizer is food for plants.
- o Blood in the veins is blue and blood in arteries is red.
- o It is cold in the winter because the Earth is farther from the Sun.

❏ Identify the misconceptions your own students exhibit by closely listening to discussions, questioning prior to investigations, using preassessments, and/or incorporating questioning probes. (→ See Resources for literature on misconceptions and Chapter 8 for more on preassessments.)

❏ Consider the possible reason for the misconception. This can be established through questioning students and connecting the responses to the literature.

❏ Provide experiences that will help students reconstruct their understanding. Addressing misconceptions directly is beneficial in the learning process. Student learning is enhanced when students directly confront an experience that contradicts their strongly held misunderstandings.

❏ Reassess along the way to determine if students have shifted their thinking and developed a scientific understanding.

Don't think you can change these misconceptions simply by telling students accurate information and explaining why they are wrong. They need experiences, and it may take several different approaches to help them change their thinking. Thus, it's important to select alternate conceptions that directly correlate to the misconception you want to address. It is critical to bring out their understanding and vocalize how their thinking changes through the experiences. The metacognition involved is essential in changing students' ideas.

Inclusion

We should not enter a classroom to teach if we don't honestly believe that those students who come through our doors are capable of learning, but we need strategies and an understanding of their needs. The position of teacher brings with it great responsibility. Accepting this responsibility requires that we avoid assuming that our students all come to us with certain prerequisite skills and understandings. Getting to know each student is the best assurance you have that you are providing for their needs.

Most schools have resources available to classroom teachers that will provide them with information concerning the learning needs of each child. Check with your department chair, mentor, or team leader to determine the types of records you may need to accomplish this. Be sure to read and understand them. If you are unclear as to how you can help a child, ask for help. It is not an indication that you are a weak teacher if you request help concerning strategies for a specific student. You are simply asking for information concerning what has been effective in the past, what strategies you might try, and how you can support this child in their learning. In some situations, the special education teacher and classroom teacher can work together in the classroom to meet the needs of children with special needs.

Jason

I am about to enter a classroom where 20% of the students have English as a second language. I have lesson materials to use in developing their English skills, but what can I do that will not take additional class time to help them?

We find ourselves facing a growing population of English language learners (ELLs) in our classrooms. It's important to help students understand what they are listening to and reading. The number of vocabulary words in science makes it a challenging subject for these students. You may be surprised to learn that some of the strategies you use for these students will also benefit other students in your class, including those with special needs:

- Make speech comprehensible.
    - Speak clearly and slowly, but not loudly.
    - Support speech with gestures.
    - Don't use general terms as substitutes for scientific terms. Use accurate and appropriate science terms.
    - Paraphrase or back up meaning by restating.
    - Avoid jargon, idioms, and figurative language.
- Make new information comprehensible.
    - Connect new ideas to prior learning or experiences.
    - Provide additional context to a story or lesson.
    - Model or act out new content.
    - Organize information visually, using graphic organizers, charts, diagrams, or photographs.
    - Provide prereading opportunities to explore phenomena—both hands-on opportunities and videos.
    - Make text comprehensible, highlighting textbooks to identify important vocabulary.

> Teach students first. Be student-centered in every decision you make. Be careful. Don't fall into focusing only on content, no matter the pressures of high success on tests.
>
> —Shayna, special education teacher

○ Provide texts at a reading level students understand.

○ Use pictures, models, specimens, artifacts, and samples to support meaning. Take advantage of online dictionaries and sources of graphics. (See Resources at the end of this chapter.)

- Make directions for assignments comprehensible.

  ○ Teach directions explicitly. This is especially critical in the area of safety.

  ○ Support oral directions visually through modeling or demonstrations.

- Allow students extra time to process meaning.

Several other strategies will support these learners:

- Everyone learns a language through speaking, so the more frequently you use discussion in small groups, the better. Be sure to place ELLs with students who will help them if they have difficulty. A good way to do this is to place the ELLs with someone who speaks both their native language and English.

- Create a word wall. As you introduce new words in science, place them in a prominent place with illustrations of the object, or label the object and put it in a visible location. You will find English-speaking children using this tool as well.

- The English language learner will benefit from writing and organizing their thoughts, labeling diagrams, and sharing information. A science notebook is an excellent format for this.

- Find a volunteer parent to record special readings in science that are particularly important to the lessons. If possible, provide your English language learners with a player and these recordings to listen to the material before it is discussed in class.

- Use graphic organizers to illustrate how ideas and objects are related to one another or to organize other ideas.

See "Boosting Science Vocabulary" (p. 88) for more on this topic.

Differentiation

Alberto

I have read a lot about differentiation. What I need now are some concrete ideas to implement in my classroom immediately. How can I modify tomorrow's lesson plan to provide more differentiation?

Carol Tomlinson is a leader in the movement to provide differentiated opportunities for students. A portion of her description of differentiated instruction includes the following: At its most basic level, differentiated instruction means "shaking up" what goes on in the classroom so that students have multiple options for taking in information (content), making sense of ideas (process), and expressing what they learn (product) (Tomlinson 1999). Teachers have provided differentiated opportunities for students for decades, but during the past few years this strategy has gained attention and momentum. Differentiation to meet the needs of all students is intentional and requires conscious effort and deliberation. However, you can begin by taking small steps and adding to your repertoire.

Each time a student is provided with extra help, more time on task, a modified assignment, or product options, differentiation is taking place. The new emphasis on this strategy has provided us with a realization of the importance of these opportunities. We need to be constantly aware of the needs of students and offer as many differentiated opportunities as possible. But these differentiated opportunities should not distract students from the learning goals or the focus and conceptual understanding you are attempting to develop.

There are several ways to differentiate. They can be used in combination with one another or as separate strategies. The following five key strategies for instruction are based on those provided by Tomlinson (1999):

- *Content:* what is taught or accessibility to the information and ideas that matter
    - Use textual materials at varying reading levels.
    - Provide organizers and anticipation guides for note-taking.
    - Use examples and illustrations based on student interests.
- *Process:* how students come to understand and "own" the knowledge, skills, and understanding
    - Vary the pacing of student work.
    - Use cooperative grouping (see the section about this topic later in this chapter).
    - Develop activities that lead to a variety of perspectives on topics.
    - Highlight critical content in the science text.
    - Segment and tier large assignments and projects.
    - Provide bookmarked internet sites at different levels of complexity for research.
- *Product:* demonstrations of what students know, understand, and are able to do
    - Develop rubrics for success based on grade-level expectations and individual student learning needs.
    - Teach students to use a range of presentation tools and products, including technology.
    - Create assessment tools that vary in type of response.
- *Effect:* student linking of thought and feeling in the classroom
    - Model respect.
    - Help students develop multiple perspectives on topics and issues.
    - Encourage equitable participation of each student.
    - Provide supported practice.
    - Allow for choice and individuality.

- *Learning environment:* classroom function, feeling, and provisioning
  - Arrange furniture for individual, small-group, and whole-group tasks.
  - Provide a variety of supplies and materials.
  - Create management techniques, procedures, and routines that vary based on tasks.
  - Make a variety of resources on the content and process available to students—both readings and manipulatives.

In addition, the following characteristics should be given special consideration in the science classroom:

- *Grouping:* Provide a variety of group opportunities, including whole group, triads, quads, and pairs, as well as individual. Select lab partners and group or team members carefully to provide the most support for students who need special help, as well as opportunities for students to go beyond the assignment when possible. When establishing groups, consider the multiple intelligences of students and provide balance.
- *Time on task:* Determine the appropriateness of the time given to complete the assignments, especially long-term assignments, projects, and labs. Some students may require more time, others less. Flexible time is a key feature in supporting students as they master particular objectives. Give additional learning opportunities to students who may complete their work before the allotted time has expired or provide them with more rigorous opportunities. Open the lab for students who may want to work before the school day begins. Provide lunchtime lab sessions as an option. (As a reminder, there should be no eating in the science lab.)
- *Learning mode:* Vary the teaching strategies in your instruction. Science labs and investigations provide the perfect venue for accommodating many learning styles. Howard Gardner (1999) identifies nine basic intelligences linked to learning styles. Each of the styles plays a role in providing differentiated opportunities for students. (→ See Online Appendix 7.1 for a summary of the nine intelligences.)

What are the things I would see in a classroom where differentiated instruction is taking place?

Sherrie

In a classroom where differentiation is taking place, you would see teacher-student connections. The teacher would pay close attention to the students, talk with them, ask their opinions, and perhaps sit with individuals or groups and listen. This then translates into understanding students and their needs.

You would also have a sense of community—the students should be working as a team and supporting one another. Different students play different roles, but they all work together and support the work toward a common goal. They should appreciate their differences and know that everyone has something to contribute to the success of everyone else.

Another characteristic of a differentiated classroom is the integrity of the curriculum. It should be rich in experiences, engaging, and not stagnant. Inquiry would be used as frequently as possible to engage students and support their development of understanding.

In a differentiated classroom, the teacher is not planning for each individual student; this would be impractical and impossible in a regular education classroom. But the teacher is considering the various learners and their strengths so that every learner has more opportunities to best construct conceptual understanding.

> One way that I am immediately able to determine if differentiation is taking place in a classroom is by looking at the products students generate from their work.
>
> —Lisa, high school principal

The Essentials in Developing Lessons

 Heather

I know that it is important to follow the most current national and state guidelines for the development of instructional materials. Where do I start?

A Framework for K–12 Science Education: Practices, Crosscutting Concepts, and Core Ideas was released in July 2011 by the National Research Council. This framework was designed to guide the development of standards to be adopted by the states. The standards are intended to then serve as a guide for the revision of all science-related curriculum, instruction, assessment, and professional development. The *Next Generation Science Standards* are projected to be released in 2012 and will be available through the National Academies. It's important to know and understand both the Framework and Standards documents, as they should inform your instructional strategies. It's not possible to provide a complete explanation of these documents in this book. However, a few elements are important for you to consider as you delve into this document yourself.

The Framework states:

The overarching goal of our framework for K–12 science education is to ensure that by the end of 12th grade, all students have some appreciation of the beauty and wonder of science; possess sufficient knowledge of science and engineering to engage in public discussions on related issues; are careful consumers of scientific and technological information related to their everyday lives; are able to continue to learn about science outside school; and have the skills to enter careers of their choice, including (but not limited to) careers in science, engineering, and technology. (NRC 2011, Executive Summary, p. 1)

The framework highlights the power of integrating understanding the ideas of science with engagement in the practices of science and is designed to build students' proficiency and appreciation for science over multiple years of school. Of particular note is the prominent place given to the ideas and practices of engineering. (NRC 2011, p. viii)

The Framework suggests that this be accomplished through a strong emphasis on the three major dimensions (see Figure 7.1).

You'll notice the emphasis on crosscutting concepts (frequently referred to as themes) and practices (what you may call skills) in the dimensions. Themes and practices are shown as being equal in importance to the disciplinary core ideas as you consider instructional strategies. You'll also notice the inclusion of engineering and technology in the core ideas. This is a significant shift that should inform your instruction. The Framework continues:

> By the end of the 12th grade, students should have gained sufficient knowledge of the practices, crosscutting concepts, and core ideas of science and engineering to engage in public discussions on science-related issues, to be critical consumers of scientific information related to their everyday lives, and to continue to learn about science throughout their lives. They should come to appreciate that science and the current scientific understanding of the world are the result of many hundreds of years of creative human endeavor. It is especially important to note that the above goals are for all students, not just those who pursue careers in science, engineering, or technology or those who continue on to higher education. (NRC 2011, p. 6)

> The Framework places emphasis on limiting the number of core ideas to be taught, teaching concepts in a continuum of learning that reflects the developmental progression of students' abilities, and integrating content (scientific explanation) and skills (practices). (NRC 2011, p. 7)

The new Framework identifies inquiry-based and problem-solving approaches to use in science instruction. The elements of inquiry are frequently identified within the document as being important components of knowledge and practice. A section of the Framework provides greater insight to this strategy in an attempt to clarify what is meant by inquiry in science. This essential component of science instruction has been shown to be an important component of all science learning experiences, beginning with preschool and extending into lifelong learning (NRC 2011).

It's clear that memorizing facts and information is not the most important skill in today's world. Facts change, and information is readily available. Students need an understanding of how to frame and answer questions, collect data, and then make sense of that data. Inquiry isn't just seeking the right answer, because often there is no right answer, but rather finding appropriate resolutions to questions and issues. What this means is that as you structure experiences for your

> I read the Framework and took notes that are essential for science and engineering instruction in my class. Those notes, along with copies of some of the charts shown in the Framework, are at my elbow as I create learning opportunities for my students.
>
> —Joclyn, grade 7 teacher

FIGURE 7.1. THE THREE DIMENSIONS OF THE FRAMEWORK

1. Scientific and Engineering Practices

1. Asking questions (for science) and defining problems (for engineering)
2. Developing and using models
3. Planning and carrying out investigations
4. Analyzing and interpreting data
5. Using mathematics and computational thinking
6. Constructing explanations (for science) and designing solutions (for engineering)
7. Engaging in argument from evidence
8. Obtaining, evaluating, and communicating information

2. Crosscutting Concepts

1. Patterns
2. Cause and effect: Mechanism and explanation
3. Scale, proportion, and quantity
4. Systems and system models
5. Energy and matter: Flows, cycles, and conservation
6. Structure and function
7. Stability and change

3. Disciplinary Core Ideas

Physical Sciences

PS 1: Matter and its interactions
PS 2: Motion and stability: Forces and interactions
PS 3: Energy
PS 4: Waves and their applications in technologies for information transfer

Life Sciences

LS 1: From molecules to organisms: Structures and processes
LS 2: Ecosystems: Interactions, energy, and dynamics
LS 3: Heredity: Inheritance and variation of traits
LS 4: Biological evolution: Unity and diversity

Earth and Space Sciences

ESS 1: Earth's place in the universe
ESS 2: Earth's systems
ESS 3: Earth and human activity

Engineering, Technology, and the Applications of Science

ETS 1: Engineering design
ETS 2: Links among engineering, technology, science, and society

Source: National Research Council (NRC). 2011. *A framework for K–12 science education: Practices, crosscutting concepts, and core ideas.* Washington, DC: National Academies Press. Executive Summary, p. 3.

students, you need to concentrate on developing practices within the context of core disciplinary ideas.

Science Reading and Writing

Is it really the job of a secondary science teacher to teach students how to read?

Jason

Unlike what students might see in a reading or English class, science resources are not usually written in a storytelling style or chronological sequence. Science text often starts with a main concept and then provides descriptions or supporting details. Science text often uses headings, subheadings, abstracts, summaries, sidebars, footnotes, and graphics. Science text uses specialized vocabulary and may be written from an expert point of view. Students may not realize reading science text can be a slower process than reading a novel or story, and rereading a section is appropriate and even encouraged.

Few students understand the importance of reading and writing in science class. The first image they have is participating in labs and being involved in hands-on experiences. But if they are to understand what real scientists do, they will learn that scientists must read and write as frequently as they conduct firsthand investigations.

Reading and writing go hand in hand. As students read, they will apply what they learn from their reading experiences to their writing. They should participate in reading and writing activities frequently in science class. Reading textual material will help verify student learning as well as provide information that cannot be acquired through inquiry and other investigations. It's an important tool in your collection of teaching strategies. However, if an older student cannot decode words, there is certainly a need for intervention by reading specialists.

Regardless of the grade level, an effective way to help students interact with text is by modeling with a "think-aloud," making your thinking and reading processes visible (and audible) to students. For example, science textbooks have many graphics supporting the content, but many students do not always see the relationships between graphics and text. Taking a little time to model how to make these connections may help students become more independent readers. Some teachers even accompany their students on a guided tour of each chapter of the textbook.

Consider preparing a textbook prereading tour through the use of an organizer, showing how textbooks are formatted to support student learning. (→ See Online Appendix 7.2 for an example.) Understanding the features of the text is the first step in being able to read it while using the publisher's built-in support system. Identify these helpful components and, most important, conduct a class discussion on how they can support learning:

- ☐ Table of contents
- ☐ Glossary
- ☐ Index
- ☐ Introduction to chapters
- ☐ Topic and subtopic headings within chapters
- ☐ Summary at the end of chapters
- ☐ References, bibliography, and citations for additional resources, such as URLs linked to the content
- ☐ Highlighting of new terms
- ☐ Nontext materials, such as graphs, charts, diagrams, and photos
- ☐ Special features of the specific text

Think beyond the textbook when you are looking for reading materials. Current news stories from newspapers, magazines, and online sources are excellent ways to connect what you are teaching in class to the real world (see Resources). Whether you assign articles or students find them in their research, students should look for specific information concerning the research or event. These elements will help them understand the value and validity of the information as they summarize what they have read:

- Source of information and date: establish credibility
- Main idea: problem, discovery, application
- Observations made and methods used
- Question that was posed or the working hypothesis
- Strategies that were used to solve a problem, move the investigation forward, or draw conclusions
- Findings (may include data summaries, charts, or graphs with interpretations)
- Theories or modifications to current theories resulting from the problem-solving process or discovery
- New questions, problems, investigations: next steps

Understanding science text also requires visual literacy. Think of the many nonlinguistic representations used in science: symbols on a weather map, the periodic table, chemical equations, water cycle, molecular diagrams, formulas, graphs, diagrams, and maps. It's important for science teachers to help students understand how these graphics have meaning and are an integral part of the language of science.

Once students have read about science, have them write about it. Summarizing what they learned, explaining the point of view they bring to an investigation, writing their ideas concerning results, or keeping a science notebook will engage them in writing about science.

Writing should be a part of every investigation. Students will record data and observations, prepare a summary of results, develop a conclusion, and present their information, either in written form or orally. Class blogs and wikis provide other opportunities for writing.

> Even a difficult concept can be presented to students if provided in understandable language they can relate to. If I can't find appropriate materials, I find articles on the web that address the concept and then modify them to meet the reading abilities of my students.
>
> —Shayna, special education teacher

> I wonder if many secondary students' reading "problems" are, in reality, a lack of guidance and experience in interacting with informational text.
>
> —Dwayne, grade 9 science teacher

Check with the language arts department or chair to determine if there is a scoring guide or rubric for informational writing. This is a best-case scenario because your students should already be familiar with it. If such a guide does not exist, perhaps you can collaborate with a language arts teacher to design such a rubric, focusing on science content. ($\rightarrow$ See Chapter 8, "Assessment Literacy," for rubrics.)

Science Notebooks

Tanya: What should be included in a science notebook to make it a useful tool?

One of the best ways to organize student ideas is through the use of science notebooks. Although you may initially think the purpose of a notebook is to integrate reading and writing into science, it does that and much more. It chronicles student learning and serves as a guide for students as they use it as a working document and for you as you assess their learning.

> I sometimes ask students to write their summaries as tweets (140 characters) or as haiku poems.
>
> —Joclyn, grade 7 science teacher

Your concept of a science notebook might be a folder or binder to hold reports, handouts, classwork, tests and quizzes, or other class materials. This may be accompanied by a checklist used for grading the notebook, usually indicating the precise order in which each item must appear. However, personalizing the notebook and making it a valuable learning tool will support the use of notebooking strategies and students will recognize the value.

Many teachers are working with their students to create a more useful and personalized notebook, one that will be used daily throughout the year. These teachers recognize the importance of helping their students learn organizational strategies, but they also recognize the importance of helping students become better at recording and analyzing data and using writing to reflect on and communicate what they are thinking and learning. These notebooks are living documents in which students keep records of their lab investigations, vocabulary, class notes, ideas, questions, sketches, summaries, and other assignments.

To make a science notebook a valuable tool for both you and the students, it must have some structure. There are many components that should be considered before you ask students to begin making entries, including your purpose in asking students to prepare a science notebook and how you will evaluate their work. ($\rightarrow$ See Resources and Online Appendix 7.3 for a sample notebook rubric.)

Depending on your purpose and how you will assess the notebooks, consider the following questions:

- What type of notebook should students use? For management purposes and grading, you will find that it is best to have the entire class use the same type of notebook in which papers can be fastened or pasted securely. Three-ring binders, spiral notebooks, composition books, grid paper composition books, or folders with prongs are options.

- What information should each notebook entry contain? The entry should be consistent and authentic. Scientists enter the date, time, and location with each entry. Weather conditions and/or location may also be an important factor. Consider the type of heading that should be included with each entry. (You may want to go online and find samples of scientists' notebooks to illustrate how they keep records.)

- What types of organizational entries should be included? Set aside a few pages in the front for a table of contents. Pages at the back can be used for a glossary. These pages will be dynamic, with entries being made each time you use the notebooks.

- What is the purpose of the notebook? Make this clear to students. A statement should be made concerning how notebooks will be used. This is actually an opportunity for student input. Ask how they would like to use their notebooks and what would benefit them the most. Consider if the notebooks will be used only for classroom investigations or if students can make additional entries. Some teachers encourage students to use their notebooks during tests, especially for essay questions.

- What types of entries should students include? What will support their learning of science, reading, and writing? Naturally students should be writing about what they have discovered but consider how they will lay out their information and represent it. Can they use quick notes and lists, or do you want only complete sentences and fully developed paragraphs? Are some elements appropriate at some time while others are not? Consider graphs, tables, charts, diagrams with labels, rubbings, photos, small samples adhered with tape, and/or use of color and keys. Do you want them to use a specific format for expressing their information? Consider including these components for each investigation:
  - The question, problem, and/or purpose of the investigation
  - Students' prediction of the outcome or a hypothesis
  - A plan for how students will conduct their research
  - Observations, both qualitative and quantitative
  - Claims and evidence to support the claims
  - Conclusions based on data
  - Reflection and consideration of the next steps

- How will you assess science notebooks? Design a rubric prior to beginning the use of science notebooks. The rubric will provide you with valuable insight as to how you should direct students in creating their notebooks. Share the rubric with students to provide them with a sense of how you will assess them and how they can assess themselves.

Once students begin using science notebooks, it is critical that you support them and encourage them to use their entries. In class discussions, ask students to reference what they have written. Ask them to share specific data they have collected and draw conclusions based on that data. Have students read aloud entries they have made and share illustrations they have included.

> My students did not catch on to my approach to notebooks right away because they have had many years of explicit directions on exactly what papers and information to archive. I had to provide lots of modeling, feedback, and persistence to get to the point where students see notebooks as a useful and integral part of their science classes.
>
> —Pat, grade 11 science teacher

Boosting Science Vocabulary

There are so many terms for students to learn in science. How can I help them learn these words and the definitions?

Alberto

Developing a working vocabulary in science is essential. A working vocabulary is not only important as students read science materials but also vital for students to communicate with one another. This can be a huge task. Many high school texts may have more than 3,000 specialized terms. There are several strategies that can support students as they learn new vocabulary. Begin by making the quantity manageable.

- Distill the new terms provided in the textbook to words that are essential: those important to understanding the unit's essential concepts, those applicable to other units, and those specifically mentioned in the standards. Have students prioritize the terms in their learning strategies. You could also have a supplemental list of "nice to know" words and words students should already know. For example, in a unit on plants at the upper-elementary level, *photosynthesis* may be an essential term. At the secondary level, *photosynthesis* could be on the review list.
- Focus on vocabulary prior to reading. When possible, link the new term to an experiment, diagram, demonstration, piece of equipment, or prior learning experience. Require students to include new terms in the glossary of their science notebooks.
- Make dictionaries available. If possible, have a dictionary on each desk during reading assignments. Teach students to use the dictionary when they encounter the first unknown word. Skipping unknown words in hopes of defining them through context reduces science literacy.
- Have students create flash cards for new vocabulary. Put the term on the front and the definition and a sentence or representative diagram on the back. Other information that links this term to prior or concurrent learning may be included as well. Conduct a flash card activity. Have students create categories and sort their flash cards of both new and mastered vocabulary. As an alternative, use a word splash or word sort (→ see Online Appendix 7.4).
- Teach students to look for key terms that imply relationships between variables or concepts. Words such as *since, when, affect, consequently, although, effect, if,* and *because* signal the discussion of related variables.
- Create a word wall. Assign each student one of the new terms in turn, have them determine a definition for the word within the context of current studies, and post the word and its meaning on a designated section of a bulletin board. Extend this learning by having the student also post a picture, diagram, photo, or other visual to represent the word.

You may think students know how to recall terms and their meaning. In some cases, they may need to memorize information due to its specific nature. Teach them how to do this but also provide them with the time and tools to recall the terms.

—Dwayne, grade 9 science teacher

- Have the class say the word aloud. This may sound like something reserved for lower elementary grades, but it is very effective, especially with science terms that may be difficult to pronounce. Clap out the syllables for long, unfamiliar words (e.g., *photosynthesis* or *thermodynamics*).
- Use new words frequently in multiple accurate contexts and encourage students to use the word as well.
- Create graphic organizers indicating how terms are related to each other and to the topic you are currently studying.
- Use a think-aloud to model how to use context cues to figure out what a word means. Show students the prefixes, suffixes, and root words they will see frequently in science, such as *uni-, -ology, anthrop-, bio-, cosm-,* and *ec-.* (→ For an extensive list of prefixes and suffixes, check the internet sites suggested in Resources at the end of this chapter.)

Science Projects

Long-term projects cause a dilemma. They can require you to give up a great deal of class time. However, if project work is sent home, the risk is twofold: (1) Students may procrastinate and not complete the work to the best of their ability and on time, or (2) parents may become too involved in the project, to the point that it doesn't reflect what students have learned (or some students may not have any support at home). Weighing these two issues is important as you consider selecting long-term projects for students to complete outside of class.

> Tanya
>
> I know there are a lot of benefits of engaging students in long-term investigations and projects. But, how do I overcome all of the problems that ensue when students work on projects at home? How can I structure the assignment for student success?

There is much to be learned in addition to content through project work. Project work accomplishes the following goals:

- Integrates almost every skill students use in science
- Develops students' creativity
- Provides experience in documenting, collecting, and analyzing data
- Provides experience in making oral and written presentations
- Provides a realistic experience for how science is conducted
- Develops students' tenacity, confidence, and competence
- Increases students' self esteem
- Helps students consider a career.
- Demonstrates that science is fun

- Provides a basis for further research
- Gives students the opportunity to develop a science fair project to include on college applications

If you decide the gains in project involvement outweigh the problems, the next goal is to make the project engaging and relevant to your learning goals. Science projects take a lot of teacher time. You can't simply assign a project and step away. Students need your help. The most critical time is in the beginning, when you need to provide students with clear guidelines and create a rubric that can guide them as well as help you assess their work. (→ See Online Appendix 7.5 for Science Fair Project/Research Paper Rubric.) Students will need to know how to do the following:

- Get started by developing a question to investigate
- Conduct background research on the topic
- Construct a hypothesis or an idea as to what will happen as they test their ideas
- Conduct safe investigations
- Test the hypothesis or idea
- Collect and represent data
- Analyze data and draw a conclusion based on the data
- Communicate results

Projects can be part of your curriculum and may not require a formal presentation, or you can have students share their work and participate in fairs or competitions. If the project is for a formal science fair or competition, students will also need to follow the established guidelines and be prepared to formally present their project and respond to questions posed by the judges. This may require some coaching. Some fairs and competitions provide cash prizes and/or scholarships as rewards for quality work (see resources list).

Cooperative Learning Groups

Cooperative groups are a perfect strategy for use in science classrooms at all grade levels. It is a practice for placing students in groups and having them work together to complete assignments. However, many educators find that overuse of cooperative learning can lead to boredom and conflict between students based on some students not doing their share in supporting the group. By carefully selecting students for each role within the group, you can frequently avoid that issue. This is a way to keep all students involved and tap into the strengths of each child.

Although group work has been a part of science instruction for decades, Johnson, Johnson, and Holubec (1991) formalized the concept and provided the following criteria for effective cooperative learning:

- Students understand that their membership in a learning group means they either succeed or fail—together.

> I have found it beneficial to send home an explanation of any long-term project assigned to my students. A part of the explanation includes a request that parents not do the work for their child. I have actually asked the parents to sign this paper and send it back to me as an agreement to provide the child with minimal help.
>
> —Dale, grade 3 teacher

- Positive interdependence includes mutual goals, joint rewards, resource interdependence (each group member has different resources that must be combined to complete the assignment), and role interdependence (each group member is assigned a specific role).
- Students help each other learn and encourage individual team members' success.
- Individuals in the group understand that they are accountable to each other and to the group as a distinct unit.
- Interpersonal and small-group skills are in place, including communication, decision making, conflict resolution, and time management.
- Members are aware of the group's processes. Individual members talk about the group as a unique entity.

Grouping students to work collaboratively and cooperatively offers benefits for learners. Teachers who are successful at facilitating cooperative learning use a variety of strategies as they create groups and design experiences:

- Create the right type of group for the need. Formal cooperative groups are not always necessary. Sometimes an occasional informal ad hoc group is needed, such as pair and share.
- Keep group size small. Ideally, learning groups include no more than four students. Groups may be larger based on the type of activity. However, a group with more than six students becomes less manageable. Consider the size of your lab tables too.
- Use ability grouping sparingly. Students, especially low-ability students, benefit by heterogeneous grouping.
- Arrange the room so that groups can work together without disrupting other groups.
- Design a rubric or grade sheet that can be used by the group and individuals to monitor their own work. Make it clear that the group will receive a grade for their work and individuals will also receive a grade for their contributions to the group and the final product.
- Don't use cooperative learning for all instructional goals. While cooperative learning is a powerful strategy, it can be overused or not applied correctly. Don't falsely manipulate an investigation that is ideal for lab partners or individuals to accomplish; select the strategy to fit the need rather than trying to make everything a cooperative effort.
- Use a variety of strategies when choosing students for groups. Many selection strategies (common clothing, favorite colors, letters in names, birthdays) will work when attempting to randomly group students. However, some students must be carefully placed for their personal success and the success of the group. Consider learning styles in establishing groups and to bring students' individual strengths to their work team (see "Differentiation" earlier in this chapter).
- Facilitate success. Predict the needs of your student groups. Develop tools and forms for their use. Have all materials ready and easily accessible.

> Allowing students to select their own partners is not usually the best way to select teams. To engage all of the students in the classroom, the teams must be carefully crafted to meet the needs of all.
>
> —Ty, middle school principal

- Support your student groups. You cannot simply set up groups and expect success. They require your support. Model specific skills before grouping students, define criteria for success, and develop rubrics for key expectations. Monitor student behavior. Circulate around the room to listen and observe groups in action. Give feedback to each group about how well the members worked with one another and accomplished tasks and how they could improve.

There are many roles students may be given as members of a cooperative group. You should establish small working groups of approximately four students. Assign students a role, but be sure all students have an opportunity to fulfill a variety of roles during the year. Provide clear directions as to what each role involves:

- The Communicator helps resolve problems. This is usually the only member of the group allowed to leave the group to ask clarifying questions of the teacher.
- The Materials Manager picks up and returns all materials needed for the investigation and is responsible for the inventory and condition of materials.
- The Checker makes sure that everyone understands their roles and what the end result should be for the project and clarifies the activity for those who don't understand.
- The Assessor or Tracker evaluates the progress at each session and tracks progress.

You may also consider the following and how they fit with your instruction and the type of activity you are conducting:

- The Organizer provides the group with overall process structure.
- The Recorder writes down the important information discussed in the group.
- The Questioner generates questions for all to answer.
- The Encourager models and reinforces social skills.
- The Summarizer restates the team's conclusions or answers.
- The Spokesperson represents the group to the entire class.
- The Timekeeper keeps everyone on task and within time constraints.
- The Team Facilitator moderates discussions, keeps the team on schedule, ensures that all members complete their work, and makes sure all students in the group have the opportunity to participate and learn.

I am interested in setting up cooperative groups. Can I use the same group for the entire year or how frequently should groups change?

Jason

You may want to change your groups frequently. Changing groups for each activity allows students to get to know others, and students also learn that if they don't get along, it doesn't matter—the group will change for the next activity. This generally means that students will work out the problem and continue their productive work because they know the situation is not permanent. You may want to keep the groups intact for a unit of study.

Answering "Why Do We Have to Learn This?"

It's easy to answer the question, "Why do I need to learn this?" with a quick response such as "because you can," "because you may need this information at some point in the future," or "because you are capable"—there are many positive responses. Responding with "because I say so" or "because it's on the test" may not motivate students. Even more logical explanations—such as "because you may decide at some time in the future to pursue a career path that right now is the last thing on Earth that you see yourself doing" or "the more knowledge and mental tools you have, the better off you will be when you present yourself to a prospective employer"—will not convince them.

Alberto

When I taught high school biology, students didn't ask me why they had to learn information about the human body. But now that I'm teaching at the middle school, I find that students ask me why they must learn specific information. How can I respond with something that makes sense rather than saying they must learn it to pass the test?

The real answer to this question is to provide experiences for students that are applicable to their lives. If the connection is not readily identifiable, then make the connections for them:

- Begin by asking yourself why that particular topic is worthy of investigation and learning.
- Consider how you can make the topic more interesting.
- Create a lesson based on what students already know.
- Structure the experience in such a way that it connects directly to real-life events or other subject areas.
- Find ways to help students personalize the process or product.

Look again at the strategies suggested in the section of this chapter about motivation. Never underestimate the effect your enthusiasm has on your students' attitudes toward a science topic and how they value it.

Teaching Study Strategies

Don't assume your students know how to study. Even a high school senior may need guidance in how to study for your class. Be specific with strategies based on the science content you are teaching and the assignments students are given. (→ See Online Appendix 7.6, "Student Guide for Learning.")

How can I support the learning that takes place at home as students are doing their homework?

Tanya

There are some quick learning strategies students may use immediately. However, they will more than likely need some modeling or direct instruction in how to make these strategies work for them within the context of a specific assignment:

> I post one of the strategies my students have been introduced to on my website along with each assignment. Providing this gives students a hint as to what they might do, and it assures me that they are being asked to use many strategies throughout the year.
>
> —Joclyn, grade 7 teacher

- Make flashcards and then practice with them.
- Read and reread.
- Highlight your notes.
- Summarize.
- Read your notes.
- Read your notes aloud.
- Organize your papers and materials so you are working with everything you need.
- Outline or make a graphic version of written work (lists, columns, Venn diagram).
- Create a visual to help you recall the facts.
- Quiz yourself or have a friend or parent quiz you.
- Write or say memory work over and over until you feel confident.
- Look over old quizzes and try to figure out why you made mistakes.
- Look over the returned assignments for the unit.
- Answer study guide questions in the text even if not assigned.
- Tell someone else what the topic is about.
- Look up the parts of the assignments that you didn't understand the first time.

You will probably see that some of the suggestions should be taught directly in class. Conduct a simple survey to determine if students feel they are capable of taking advantage of the suggestions on their own. Perhaps you'll want to support them with class time to build their skills. The time and effort will pay off in students' success.

Field Trips

Field trips can be rich experiences that add a great deal to your instruction. Field trips have multiple benefits, including the following:

- They provide students with a different method of learning. This is particularly important when we consider tactile and kinesthetic learners.
- They broaden students' ideas about how things work and expose them to topics not generally covered in science class.
- They reinforce concepts being developed in class.
- They provide experiences that can be shared and applied at a later time in the classroom.
- They help you see your students in a different environment while allowing them to see you in a different role and setting as well.

Field trips take time and planning if they are going to be successful learning opportunities. But the preparations can be worth the extra effort involved. A few steps will help ensure success. (→ See Online Appendix 7.7, "How to Set Up for a Field Trip.")

The Use of Technology

With technology we can address all different types of learning styles, provide enjoyable and interesting activities and assessments, and use multiple resources that we would not otherwise have available in the classroom. Technology also gives teachers tools for record keeping and lesson creation. Technology is changing so rapidly that anything mentioned in this book will soon be out of date. There are a few uses of technology that will play an important role in your classroom, no matter how the specific technology may change:

- Computer simulations
- Videos
- Interactive whiteboards
- Electronic portfolios
- Data collection through probes
- Enhanced senses through specialized microscopes or telescopes
- Electronic response devices
- Use of the internet for collecting information
- Record keeping

Something else that will likely not change is that classrooms will not all have enough pieces of technology for all students to use it at once. If you face this challenge, consider modifications to the way you might usually use these tools:

- Have students work in teams.
- Stagger deadlines for the final product.

> I point out a specific location at the field trip site that is easy to find and well labeled. If anyone gets lost from the group, they are to go to that location and wait for the group. A student who gets lost from the group is then my partner, and we hold hands for the rest of the day (or until someone else gets my hand). With older children, this penalty is only necessary once—they are never lost again.
>
> —Sharon, grade 5 teacher

> Some may not consider this technology. But when we didn't have a student response system available in our classrooms, we used response boards. They are made from cut panels of shower board [type of paneling used in shower that is slick and waterproof and can handle a dry-erase marker]. Each student had one and could quickly respond using a dry erase marker, hold it up for the teacher to see, and then erase it with a piece of towel. If erased immediately the marker usually doesn't leave a mark (see Resources).
>
> —Richard, science department chair

- Provide extra time before school for students who want to access tools more quickly or often.
- Have students rotate among tasks with the technology as just one component of many.
- Allow students to work on home computers for at least a portion of the assignment.
- Share tools with others in your building to create collections of specific technologies that can rotate between rooms.
- Involve the PTA, parents, and members of the community in finding ways to acquire more technology.

Finding the best ways to help students use the technology available to them to their advantage is a constant challenge. They do not always have the knowledge, resources, or skills to complete the assignments with optimum results. They may also have difficulty staying focused on the goals of the assignment and can stray into other features of the technology they are using. For these reasons, it is important to express a clear purpose for their activities, monitor them as they work, and provide direct instruction in how to use the tools properly and efficiently. Set clear expectations and rules based on your school's Acceptable Use Policy (AUP).

Class Starters and Wrap-Ups

It's important to begin class on time with an activity that engages students immediately. At the beginning of the class, have a bell-ringer (or warm-up) ready when the students come in, after you greet them at the door with a smile and greeting. They should get started right away, even before the bell actually rings, so they are engaged while you take attendance, distribute or return assignments, or check homework. This activity can also help students transition from their previous class or events that happened in the hall. Write the bell-ringer on the board or hand students a small slip of paper with the prompt as they enter the classroom. Some examples of warm-ups include the following:

- Answer a question about yesterday's work or an upcoming topic.
- Respond to a statement or visual to uncover any misconceptions, activate prior knowledge of the topic, or create connections.
- Read the introduction to an activity.
- Enter the day's learning goals into their notebooks.
- Solve a quick brainteaser or math problem.
- Complete a vocabulary entry with a graphic organizer.
- Do a quick write with several sentences on a theme or topic.
- Do a quick draw on a theme or topic.
- Put a few words on the board and ask the students to write a sentence using all of them.
- Write about this date in science history or a current event.

My students are eager to dash out the door as soon as they finish cleaning up the lab. How can I keep students from racing out of the classroom at the end of the period?

Sherrie

At the end of the class, use another bell-ringer (sometimes called an exit activity or a ticket out the door) as a formative assessment to check student understanding through a summary or brief response to a question. This also gives time to scan the room to make sure materials are put away. Exit activities get students to focus and reflect, instead of dashing from the end of one class to another without packing up their thinking. But be sure that the exit activity doesn't make students late for their next class. Exit activities have many formats:

- Adding to a notebook page
- Using a single sheet of paper divided into sections for each day or small pieces of paper (recycling old handouts) that can be turned in
- Adding to an online class blog or wiki
- Copying the day's homework assignments into a planner.

Some teachers grade bell-ringers; others include them in a class participation rubric. Some collect them and then return them at the end of the unit to review. But be sure to skim them to identify what students do or do not understand. Refer to their work the next day: *I noticed that yesterday some of you had questions about … It seems like you understand … I saw an interesting connection between …* (→ See Resources and Online Appendix 7.8 for sample bell-ringers.)

> I use the bell ringers as a part of my daily reflection. As I review the information students have provided, I am able to consider what the next step must be in their learning and then plan for the next class period based on that progression.
>
> —Dale, grade 3 teacher

Preparing for a Substitute

There was nothing in my undergraduate work that gave me ideas about what to provide for a substitute. I want to be ready for this situation. What instructional materials do I need to provide for a sub?

Jason

First-year teachers often take more sick days than veteran teachers. You will catch bugs from your students and be ill frequently until you build up an immunity to all of those germs. So, be prepared. Create backup materials for use by a substitute and leave them in a location that is easily found. If you can't leave them on your desk each day after school, put them in a place known by a colleague who can direct a substitute to them. Some schools require you to leave plans in the front office. Be sure these plans will be germane for a long period of time; revisit the file and update the materials as needed. Here are a few tips:

- Don't leave students with busy work. Provide them with something that will count and move them forward in their learning. Silent readings, doing homework, and quietly talking to one another are all exercises you cannot expect students to learn from and can easily escalate into discipline issues.
- Don't engage the students in a lab while you are away. The great benefit of observing students in a lab is that you gain insight into their learning. If you aren't there, then you don't know what they have learned and how they interacted with the materials and one another. Safety should be a primary concern, and you should not depend on a substitute to know all of the hazards of your labs.
- Make the work as engaging as possible. Perhaps provide an opportunity for pair and share or a group product to be created by the end of class.
- Don't assume the substitute has a background in science. Prepare materials with explanations that a generalist can follow as well.
- Use a video only if it applies to your current unit of study and will help with student understanding. This is the most overused strategy left in the hands of a substitute. If you leave them a video, then also leave a post-video discussion guide or student response form.
- Be sure to include all the information a sub may need in your substitute file.

Remember, part of being a professional is preparing for those times when you cannot be with your class. You are evaluated on all of your work, including the provisions you make when you are not in attendance. (→ See Chapter 4 for more on preparing for a substitute.)

Homework

 What do I use as a guideline to determine if I should assign homework?

Sherrie

A critical component of planning lessons is the development of homework. Consider why you assign homework. What purpose does it fill in your overall teaching strategy? You have so little time with your students in class, and homework is one way to extend the amount of time available. However, you must be careful in preparing homework assignments so they are meaningful and students can accomplish what you ask them to do. They may have an assignment that is in a familiar format they can attack easily. However, it may be a topic or format that is not familiar. In that case, it is important to provide class time for students to begin the work. By walking around the room and checking on students, you can help them find the correct path quickly while also developing an understanding concerning their needs.

> One of my favorite vocabulary activities for a substitute is a word splash. [→ See Online Appendix 7.4.]
>
> —Dwayne, grade 9 science teacher

> Students who chose not to do their work are signaling the teacher for help.
>
> —Sharon, grade 5 teacher

As you design homework or class work to be completed at home, follow these steps:

- ❐ Determine what you want the students to accomplish.
- ❐ Prepare a document or assignment that includes all of the steps you want students to accomplish.
- ❐ Provide directions and questions in simple language that can be easily followed (you won't be there to clarify).
- ❐ Consider how you will evaluate the homework.
- ❐ Make the due date realistic based on the amount of time it will require. Perhaps it isn't due until the end of the week.

There is a constant debate in the American education system about the value of homework. Much of the issue is based on the piles of homework students are expected to complete. Don't give homework just to keep students busy. It should have purpose and relate to the concepts you are developing in class. If you are wondering about the amount of homework to provide, check with your mentor. Some schools have guidelines that may restrict the number of minutes of homework per day or week.

> I think that if you are assigning students to read the chapter and answer the questions at the end on a regular basis, you should rethink your homework assignments.
>
> —Joclyn, grade 7 science teacher

Conclusion

Once you have had an opportunity to teach using all of your newfound strategies and students have become active learners, your next step is to assess their understanding. But you must consider how and what you will assess before you even begin the process of teaching. That makes the next chapter in this book an important companion to what you have learned in this chapter.

Resources *(www.nsta.org/riseandshine)*

Cooperative Learning Groups

Cooperative Learning: *http://edtech.kennesaw.edu/intech/cooperativelearning.htm.* This site includes information about the Johnson and Johnson model while also providing strategies to use in the groups, such as think-pair-share, three-step interview, and round-robin brainstorming.

Developing Lessons

American Association for the Advancement of Science (AAAS). 2001. *Atlas of science literacy.* Washington, DC: American Association for the Advancement of Science, Project 2061.

Bransford, J. A., A. Brown, and R. Cocking, eds. 1999. *How people learn: Brain, mind, experience, and school.* Washington, DC: National Academies Press. *www. nap.edu/openbook.php?isbn=0309070368*

Duschl, R. A., H. A. Schweingruber, and A. W. Shouse, eds. 2007. *Taking science to school: Learning and teaching in grades K–8.* Washington, DC: National Academies Press. *www.nap.edu/openbook.php?record_id=11625*

National Research Council (NRC). 2000. *Inquiry and the national science education standards: A guide for teaching and learning.* Washington, DC: National Academies Press. *http://books.nap.edu/catalog.php?record_id=9596*

Differentiation

Gregory, G. H. 2008. *Differentiated instructional strategies for science, grades K–8.* Thousand Oaks, CA: Corwin Press.

Discrepant Events

Discrepant Events: *www.plu.edu/~vedrosr/discrepant.html.* This site has a variety of discrepant events that are used not only as demonstrations but also as student activities.

Koballa Jr., T. R. The Motivational Power of Science Discrepant Events. *http://bcramond.myweb.uga.edu/home/DiscrepantEvents.htm.* You will find discrepant events in several categories, as well as an excellent brief explanation of research involving the use of this strategy with students.

O'Brien, T. 2010. *Brain-powered science: Teaching and learning with discrepant events.* Arlington, VA: NSTA Press.

O'Brien, T. 2011. *Even more brain-powered science: Teaching and learning with discrepant events.* Arlington, VA: NSTA Press.

O'Brien, T. 2011. *More brain-powered science: Teaching and learning with discrepant events.* Arlington, VA: NSTA Press.

Whelmers: *www.mcrel.org/whelmers/index.asp.* Whelmers are tools to be used by a classroom teacher to engage students and draw their attention from the incredibly busy and hurried lifestyle we all experience. This site, from McREL's Accessible Science Series, has a variety of whelmers on many science topics.

Field Trips

Froschauer, L. ed. 2008. *Science beyond the classroom: An NSTA Press journals collection.* Arlington, VA: NSTA Press.

Russell, H. R. 2001. *Ten-minute field trips: A teacher's guide to using the school grounds for environmental studies.* 3rd ed. Arlington, VA: NSTA Press.

Misconceptions

"Easier to Address" Earth Science Misconceptions: *http://serc.carleton.edu/NAGTWorkshops/intro/misconception_list.html.* These misconceptions are organized in several categories in geoscience, including Earth's structure, plate tectonics, and earthquakes.

Earth Science Misconceptions: *http://k12s.phast.umass.edu/~nasa/misconceptions.html.* Misconceptions are provided here in a chart form.

Exploring and Dealing with Students' Alternative Conceptions: *http://cstl-csm.semo.edu/waterman/SE320AltCert/protected/alternativeconc.html.* Myths about the nature of science, textbook misconceptions, and general alternative conceptions are identified on this site, along with misconceptions in science content areas. By clicking some of the links, you will find many more misconceptions resources.

Notebooking

Campbell, B., and L. Fulton. 2003. *Science notebooks: Writing about inquiry.* Portsmouth, NH: Heinemann.

Fulwiler, B. R. 2007. *Writing in science: How to scaffold to support learning.* Portsmouth, NH: Heinemann.

Marcarelli, K. 2010. *Teaching science with interactive notebooks.* Thousand Oaks, CA: Corwin Press.

Science Notebooks in K–12 Classrooms: *www.sciencenotebooks.org.* This site provides an introduction to science notebooks, suggestions for features you may want to include in a notebook, a database of searchable examples of student work, classroom tools including lessons, and teacher resources. It is the go-to place to get started in designing your science notebook.

Science Notebooks: Tools For Increasing Achievement Across the Curriculum: *www. ericdigests.org/2004-4/notebooks.htm.* A review of the literature and guidelines for how to use science notebooks are features of this article.

Using Science Notebooks K–8: *www.tusd1.org/contents/depart/science/notebook.asp.* This Regional Science Center provides a glimpse into what one school system is doing to include the use of science notebooks as an instructional tool. The site includes a working definition for science notebooks, explains the purpose for using this tool, and provides resources.

Reading

Barton, M. L., and D. L. Jordan. 2001. *Teaching reading in science.* Aurora, CO: Mid-Continent Research for Education and Learning. Companion to Billmyer and Barton (1998).

Billmyer, R., and M. L. Barton. 1998. *Teaching reading in the content areas: If not me, then who?* Alexandria, VA: Association for Supervision and Curriculum Development.

English Language Roots: Word Prefixes, Suffixes & Syllables: *www.prefixsuffix.com.* The use and meaning of prefixes and suffixes

The Internet Picture Dictionary: *www.pdictionary.com*

TweenTribune: *http://tweentribune.com/join.* Engage, inform, and educate your students with TweenTribune and TeenTribune. These sites let students interact with the news while fulfilling requirements for language arts, computer skills, and other classes. Each weekday, TweenTribune scours the Web for age-appropriate news stories that will interest tweens and teens and invites them to comment. All comments are moderated by their teachers before they are published. (The entire website is in both English and Spanish.) You and your students must sign up for this site.

Vasquez, J., M. Comer, and F. Troutman. 2010. *Developing visual literacy in science K–8.* Arlington, VA: NSTA Press.

Rubrics

Assessing Projects: Demonstrating Understanding Rubrics and Scoring Guides: *http://www97.intel.com/pk/AssessingProjects/AssessmentStrategies/Demon-stratingUnderstanding/ap_rubrics_scoring_guides.htm.* Most of the major student science fairs and competitions have scoring guidelines available online. This one is from Intel.

Doran, R., F. Chan, and P. Tamir. *Science educator's guide to laboratory assessment.* Arlington, VA: NSTA Press.

iRubric: *www.iRubric.com.* You are required to register to use this site, but it is well worth the effort. You'll find a variety of ready-to-use rubrics on many topics organized by grade level, subject, and type. At last count, there were more than 154,000 rubrics in the public gallery. Don't be intimidated—it has a powerful search engine. You can use them as they are or modify in any way you would like.

Lantz, H. B. 2004. *Rubrics for assessing student achievement in science grades K–12.* Thousand Oaks, CA. Sage Publications.

RubiStar: *http://rubistar.4teachers.org.* All sorts of information about rubrics can be found on this site, including background, a tutorial, and suggestions for rubric development. Create your own rubric based on topics such as oral projects, products, multimedia, research and writing, work skills, and science topics.

Writing Rubrics: *www.rubrics4teachers.com/writing.php.* A variety of completed writing rubrics are available at this site, including topics such as compare and contrast, narrative writing, reflective writing, position paper writing, writing to describe, and writing to inform.

Science Fairs

National Science Teachers Association (NSTA). 2003. *Science fairs plus: Reinventing an old favorite: An NSTA Press journals collection.* Arlington, VA: NSTA Press.

Technology

Edmodo: *http://Edmodo.com.* This site provides social learning for classrooms. Create a group, give students a special code to access it, and then share information. Hand out, manage, and grade assignments. There is a location to post lessons, ideas, and files to share with other teachers. The ways that students and teachers interact with technology outside the classroom affects what happens in the classroom. You will need to sign up, but there is no fee. This user-friendly site provides a tutorial to get you started, as well as clips of classroom teachers using Edmodo with their students.

Making and Using Whiteboards in the Classroom: *www.edufy.org/content/show/499.* Tips for how to use dry-erase response boards in your classroom.

PhET Interactive Simulations: *http://phet.colorado.edu.* The University of Colorado at Boulder created and updates this site. It contains research-based simulations of physical phenomenon. This site is ideal to use on interactive boards and is organized by type, grade level, and content, and even has simulations in several languages.

Promethean Planet: *www.prometheanplanet.com/en.* "The World's Largest Interactive Whiteboard Community" is the tagline for this site. The site offers professional development, resources, a discussion community, and support for those who own the product.

Wetzel, D. R. 2005. *How to weave the web into K–8 science.* Arlington, VA: NSTA Press. This book is a guide for how to bring the internet into your classroom.

Online Appendixes

7.1 Summary of Gardner's Nine Intelligences

7.2 Textbook Prereading Organizer

7.3 Science Notebook Rubric

7.4 Word Splash

7.5 Science Fair Project and Research Paper Rubric

7.6 Student Guide for Learning

7.7 How to Set Up for a Field Trip

7.8 Idea for Bell Ringers

CHAPTER 8
ASSESSMENT LITERACY

Jason

Dear Ms. Mentor,

I want to use more essay-type questions on my unit assessments, but with 150 students, I feel swamped trying to grade all of the papers and provide feedback. Do you have suggestions for making this a good learning process?

Dear Jason,

Sitting at your desk for hours after giving a test seems like a monumental task. But there are things you can do to keep your sanity.

Determine the purpose of your test questions. Making lists and writing definitions are low-level tasks that could be assessed with objective or short-answer questions. Use essay questions to find out how well students can describe, analyze, summarize, compare and contrast, identify advantages and disadvantages, create a graphic, interpret data, or address what if or why questions.

There may be many correct responses to these higher-level questions. Make a rubric in advance to describe what a great response, a satisfactory one, and an incomplete one would include. I used a version of the rubric my state had for writing, with an emphasis on the content of the response.

It may be helpful to have students do more writing in class, where you can model and provide immediate feedback. Share some sample questions and your basic rubric with the students ahead of time, along with examples of responses at each of the levels. Students can practice writing in their notebooks or share their work with classmates.

Explain to students that you need time to read their work carefully and respond thoughtfully. I divided tests into two parts: objective and essay. The objective part I could return and discuss quickly (even the next day), but the essays I returned and discussed a little later. I also had a separate score for each part, showing students the essays were just as important as the objective questions.

If you're using a paper test, ask students to start each essay response at the top of a separate page, even if their previous response did not take up a whole side. You can then organize the papers so that you are reading all of the responses to question 1 first, followed by the responses to question 2, and so on. This way your rubric for each question is fresh in your mind, and after a few papers you will get the general gist of how students are responding.

Now that you're streamlining the process, you should have time to provide feedback. Feedback should be more than a final grade or total score and more than a generic "good job" or "needs work" comment. To be effective, feedback should be focused on the task to provide comments on what was good and suggestions for improvement, such as "Your description used vocabulary that helped me visualize the process" or "Add two or three additional details for a more complete description."

Most important, don't give up! In real life, few of us take multiple-choice tests for a living. But we do write notes, memos, summaries, letters, articles, and blogs. So anything we can do to help students become better thinkers and writers is worth the time and effort.

—Ms. Mentor

STUDENT LEARNING IS the ultimate goal of everything you do in the classroom. Assessment is the process of gathering information (or evidence) from a variety of sources to determine what students are learning in terms of knowledge and skills and how they can apply their learning to problem-solving or creative situations. Assessments can also provide feedback on the effectiveness of your learning goals, instructional strategies, and choice of instructional materials. (→ See Chapter 7, "Teaching Strategies.")

Although a comprehensive discussion of assessments and grading is beyond the scope of this book, this chapter provides some information and ideas that will prove helpful to the beginning teacher.

Purpose of Assessments

> **Tanya**
> *Is an assessment the same as a test?*

Many types of activities in science—lab reports, quizzes, unit tests, projects, presentations, science notebooks, and other assignments (e.g., vocabulary, chapter questions, problems)—can be used as assessments if you do more than check off that students completed it. Analyzing these activities can give you a more complete picture of what students are learning and their progress toward achieving the learning goals. Looking at student work can also provide feedback on the effectiveness of instructional strategies. (→ See Online Appendixes 6.2 and 8.1 for suggestions on grading and evaluating student work.)

Unfortunately, many teachers, administrators, parents, and students view assessments as separate from the learning process. They may consider tests and other assignments as a way of collecting points in order for the teacher to compute a grade.

Your assignments and assessments should be carefully aligned with the learning goals. In this book, the term *learning goals* is used to describe what students are expected to learn. Some schools may use other terms, including *objectives, outcomes,* or *expectations*.

Ideally, assessments are designed or selected as you identify the learning goals. Assessments can occur throughout the learning unit: prior to instruction, during the learning activities, and at the end of the unit. The type of assessment you use should relate to its purpose.

> For each learning goal, I indicate in my lesson plan the possible activities students can perform to demonstrate their learning.
>
> —Dwayne, grade 9 science teacher

Preassessments

> **Alberto**
> *I don't have time to create a pretest for each unit. In what other ways could I find out what students already know?*

Preassessments can be used to learn what knowledge, skills, and experiences students bring to the learning unit. Assessing students' prior knowledge can also identify misconceptions or incomplete understandings. The results of any preassessments should not be factored into the students' grades.

If students are already familiar with a topic, you won't need to spend a lot of time reteaching the basics, other than perhaps a brief review. You can develop activities and topics that are more in-depth and extend the students' knowledge and experiences. However, if students do not have the background knowledge and skills you expected, you'll need activities that introduce students to fundamental concepts and processes. Preassessments have a variety of formats:

- Traditional pretests contain items similar to what would appear on the unit tests. Some students find these frustrating, however, because they might not know many of the answers. You can reassure students that this does not count as a grade and have students compare their pretest and unit test scores to chart their own learning.
- Probes are brief activities that are based on specific content and help teachers identify students' preconceptions or misconceptions about the topic (Keeley, Eberle, and Farrin 2005).
- KWL charts are three-column graphic organizers on which students note what they already know (K) about a topic, what they want (W) to know, and finally what they learn (L) about a topic. The K and W columns can provide information prior to instruction. (→ See Resources and Online Appendixes 8.2a–c for examples of KWL charts.)
- In a free-write or as a prompt to a visual, ask students to list what they know about a topic. As with a KWL chart, students can include what they've learned about a topic from a variety of sources, including what they may have learned outside of school.
- On a list of key vocabulary or concepts, ask students to put a plus sign next to those they're comfortable with, a check mark next to those they've heard of but are unsure about, and a question mark next to those with which they are completely unfamiliar.

The curriculum of a previous course or grade level could help you determine what topics may have already been covered or what activities students may have done. This is no guarantee of what students actually learned, however. Sometimes students claim to be unfamiliar with a topic. These preassessments may refresh their memories as they dig into their prior knowledge.

Preassessments can also be helpful in differentiated instruction (→ see Chapter 7 for more on differentiation). Once you identify what experiences and knowledge students have, you can plan activities for those who need basic instruction and those who are ready for more advanced work.

Formative Assessments

Formative assessments are frequent, ongoing, classroom-level assessments used to discover what students are learning during the instructional process. They are often referred to as assessments *for* learning. Based on the results, students can move on if they've learned a topic, or you can revisit and revise your instruction to correct any misunderstandings or fill in any gaps.

Some of my students said they had never heard of mitosis before. My preassessment showed that another teacher had used the term cell division instead of mitosis, so the students knew more than what they thought—just in different words.

—Richard, science department chair

Heather

Do formative assessments take time away from instruction? When will I have time to teach?

Formative assessments can be varied so they become an integral and enjoyable part of the learning process. They are usually not graded, so students have a chance to ask questions and reflect honestly on their learning—and not be penalized for a mistake, misconception, question, or incomplete understanding while they are learning new content or skills. You may already have activities that could be part of a formative assessment process:

- Thumbs-up or thumbs-down responses from students can give you instant feedback during a discussion or activity. You can follow up by asking a thumbs-up student to explain briefly or using some probing questions with a thumbs-down student to find out the source of the confusion (which other students may have too).
- Students write short responses on small whiteboards or half sheets of paper and hold them up. A brief scan of the room lets you see the responses and know all students are involved. This is a low-tech version of the clicker systems that allow students to respond electronically for an instant check of their understanding.
- In a variation of the think-pair-share strategy, students do a quick write in their science notebook, share their writing with a partner, and then summarize for the class. If the summaries start to sound the same after the first few, you can ask other teams if they have questions or anything new to add. As you listen to their summaries, you can get a feel for what students are learning, and the other students get to hear the information in different words or from a different perspective.
- As students complete the L column of a KWL chart to describe what they are learning, you get a glimpse into their thinking.
- You can use an observation checklist to identify content skills or lab behaviors in which students are successful and those in which they may need additional guidance or instruction. Record your observations as you walk around while students are working independently or in groups. Spend a little time with each group to observe their work, ask a few questions, or provide any clarification.
- Use an exit activity to check student understanding before they leave. Ask the students to write a brief summary or respond to a question in their science notebooks, an online blog, or a piece of paper. (→ See Chapter 7 for more on class starters and wrap-up.)
- Although you may score them, quizzes and lab reports can be used formatively, too.

I heard one time that formative assessment is the tasting a chef does in the kitchen, and summative assessment is the guests celebrating a good meal. If the chef does not do any tasting, he or she is taking a chance on whether the meal will turn out to be memorable for the guests!

—Ty, middle school principal

These strategies assume that all students are involved, you provide feedback, students have the opportunity to correct their work, and you use the results to improve or validate your instruction. Students should see these activities as part of the learning process.

Regardless of what activity you use for formative assessment, it's important for students to get feedback beyond whether their responses were correct or incorrect. Giving specific suggestions for improvement, asking probing or follow-up questions, encouraging the students to correct their mistakes, identifying student strengths, and helping students self-assess their work are part of the formative assessment process.

So what does a teacher do if the students didn't get it? It may be tempting to assume they weren't paying attention (which may be true) or to repeat the information in a louder or slower voice. But you need a few extra tricks up your sleeve to adjust your instruction:

- Alternative explanations (Ask a student who understands the concept to explain it to the others.)
- Extra practice activities that are provided in a different context (once any misunderstandings are cleared up)
- Other visuals (such as models, charts, diagrams, graphic organizers) or multimedia (such as videos or podcasts)
- Additional examples and non-examples of the concept
- Think-alouds
- Alternative readings

Of course, if all the students get it, it's time to move on to the next part of the lesson. Sometimes their understanding may be temporary, and some additional review and assessment might be necessary later.

Summative Assessments

Summative assessments are used to evaluate student performance related to the learning goals. Often called exams, the assessments usually occur after the instructional activities have taken place and are commonly used in assigning grades. Although local, state, and national standardized tests can be considered summative, the focus here is on teacher-created tests given at the end of a learning unit, semester, or academic year. In some schools, teachers of the same course will collaborate on summative assessments, especially end-of-course exams.

How do I identify which type of test items I should use?

Jason

When you're creating a summative assessment, it's important to match the type of item to your learning goals:

- Multiple-choice items to determine if students can identify or recognize concepts
- Short answer or fill-in-the-blank items to determine if students can recall concepts
- Essay questions to determine how students can describe, compare and contrast, summarize, explain, or evaluate

The best time to design a summative assessment is when you're planning the learning unit. As you write the learning goals and objectives, decide which type of item would demonstrate student learning. The number of items depends on the number and complexity of your learning goals. Many states and other agencies have sets of released items that correspond to science standards and are available to teachers. (→ See Resources for a few examples.)

You can certainly include graphics on the assessment for students to label, analyze, or describe. Avoid questions on nonessential vocabulary or concepts that were not presented in class. Do not use joke items or use an assessment to see if students remember trivial facts. And never use an assessment as a punishment for student misbehavior or inattention.

Test banks of questions are often included with a textbook's teacher resources. These may or may not align with your learning goals, so choose those that reflect the concepts and skills that were part of your instruction. Eliminate or rewrite any that contain errors or are poorly written.

At the secondary level, it can be appropriate to use answer sheets that are separate from the test questions. This saves paper, as the same tests can be reused in other sections. A single answer sheet can be easier to score than paging through an entire booklet (especially if you have several classes to assess). Younger or less-experienced students may have difficulty transitioning from the test page to an answer form. When designing assessments, include all components of a question on the same page, including graphics and the response selections. Work with the special education teachers to determine the accommodations that students may require.

In authentic assessments, students perform a real-world activity to demonstrate how they can apply their knowledge to a new task or situation (Mueller 2010). These may also be called projects, alternative assessments, or performance assessments. Characteristics of authentic assessments (Miami Museum of Science 2001) include the following:

- The project or task is usually rich in design and long term.
- The assessment task simulates real-world challenges.
- The project focuses on inquiry and investigation.
- Students are given a realistic role and use realistic resources and materials.
- Students are allowed to develop alternative solutions. There is no one right answer.

> I've heard that formative assessments are assessment *for* learning; summative assessments are assessments *of* learning.
>
> —Pat, grade 11 science teacher

Can science projects be considered a kind of assessment?

Sherrie

Authentic assessments provide opportunities for students to work both as part of a group and independently. These assessments complement traditional tests by providing opportunities for students to integrate their content knowledge, creativity, and skills in collaboration, organization, communication, and problem solving. These assessments often require a product such as a report, model, or presentation to an audience (live or via multimedia). If students are new to any of the components of authentic assessments, they will need your guidance and support.

Examples of authentic assessments include

- presentations,
- debates and panel discussions,
- inventions,
- model building and testing,
- the creation of resources for younger students,
- community service projects,
- case studies,
- simulations,
- writing for an audience,
- multimedia projects,
- exhibitions and displays, and
- research projects (e.g., science fairs).

> I've found that students who do not score well on paper-and-pencil tests may do very well on oral exams or on projects.
>
> —Shayna, special education teacher

For projects or other authentic assessments, teachers often provide students with a list of requirements or specifications to guide them. They usually have a rubric associated with them based on these requirements.

Rubrics

What are the advantages of having rubrics? Should I share them with the students?

Sherrie

Scoring objective tests is simple: The answer is either correct or incorrect. Scoring essay questions, lab reports, writing assignments, cooperative learning or group work, presentations, or other projects (including multimedia ones) is more complicated. Some students (intuitively or through prior experience) just seem to know how to do things well. Others, however, need some guidance to understand what quality work looks like.

Facing a pile of reports, a roomful of projects, or boxes of science notebooks to evaluate can be a daunting task. In the interest of time, it's tempting to concentrate on factors that are easier to grade, such as length, neatness, spelling and grammar, and whether deadlines were met. While these criteria may be important, it's more important to concentrate on the actual content knowledge and skills that students demonstrate related to the learning goals.

This is where rubrics can be useful. A rubric is a description of desired criteria, including levels of achievement for each criterion. A rubric can range from a holistic guide to a more detailed, analytic tool, written in the form of a table with levels such as excellent, proficient, basic, or beginning and a description of what work at that level would include for each criterion.

Creating rubrics can be a time-consuming task, but you don't necessarily need a brand-new rubric for each assignment. For example, a basic lab report rubric can be modified for different kinds of investigations. As your students become more accomplished, you can add additional criteria. Examining rubrics created by others will give you some ideas to use or adapt, rather than always starting from scratch. Many NSTA journal articles and NSTA Press books include rubrics for the activities or investigations and exemplify a variety of formats and criteria. The internet is another source of ideas for rubrics and tools for creating them. (→ See Resources for links to rubrics and tools.)

It may be helpful if your science department has some common rubrics, although reaching a consensus on the levels and criteria may be a challenge. It's not easy to put criteria and levels into words, but the discussions about the indicators of student learning can be enlightening. These common rubrics provide consistency across subjects, teachers, and grade levels.

Sharing the rubrics with the students ahead of time shows them how their work will be evaluated and eliminates the "guess what the teacher thinks is important" frustration many students have. Students also get feedback that is more focused than phrases such as "good job" or "try harder." As they become more familiar with rubrics, your students can help create rubrics and use them for reflection and self-assessment.

> Each classroom in the school displays a standard rubric for informational writing, based on the state's writing assessment criteria. Regardless of the subject area, the students and teachers have a consistent idea of effective writing.
>
> —Lisa, high school principal

Providing Informative Feedback

What kinds of comments would be appropriate to put on students' work?
Tanya

If students don't understand the purpose of assessments, they may think of assessments as something that happens so teachers can assign a grade at the end of a marking period. The type of feedback they get may reinforce this misconception. If all students see are red checkmarks, circles around misspelled words, and a grade at the top of the page, it's understandable when they crumple the paper or put it into a notebook without paying much attention. It's also important to provide feedback that is more informative than a smiley face or simply saying "nice work."

Research indicates that providing feedback is an effective strategy for improving student learning (Brookhart 2008). Feedback should focus on what specifically the student did well, point out where the student may have made errors or demonstrated incomplete thinking, or discuss how the student could improve. Rubrics can be used to provide feedback, but a personal remark or specific suggestions from the teacher can also be helpful to students.

Eventually, you'll develop feedback statements (such as the ones below) that can be adapted to many assignments:

- You've supported your conclusion with evidence from the lab.
- Using a diagram to compare and contrast plant and animal cells was a great idea. It helped me understand what you mean.
- By lining up the numbers in a table, you could make your data easier to understand. Please revise this table.
- Your explanation was very clear and included three supporting reasons.
- I don't understand what you mean in this paragraph. Could you please clarify?
- I enjoyed reading this because you have some creative ideas.

Should you provide feedback on grammar and spelling? It's common for rubrics to have an "effective communications" criterion that includes conventions, spelling, and legibility. But in an assessment of science learning goals, feedback on the content of the response and the use of inquiry skills should be more important considerations. You could spend hours trying to edit student work, but an abundance of corrections could discourage students from writing. You could certainly ask students to revise for legible writing, the basics of standard grammar and usage, and correct spelling of words that are essential to the unit (those on the word wall or in their notebooks). But you will have to make exceptions for students who are learning English or who have disabilities that affect their writing.

During learning activities, it's helpful for students to provide feedback to each other. How to do this effectively should be part of your guidance and modeling during cooperative learning. (→ See Chapter 7 for more on cooperative learning groups.)

> I can still remember when teachers took the time to write personal notes on my work.
>
> —Richard, science department chair

Meeting Expectations

I'm feeling really frustrated. I thought the students were following along in the unit, but I am really disappointed in the test results. What can I do differently in the next unit?

Alberto

There will be a time when students don't do as well as you would like on a summative assessment. Despite what you've heard, a large number of failing grades is not a sign of academic rigor. If the purpose of your test was to record a grade for the students, it can be tempting to curve or adjust the scores so more students receive a passing grade or to move on to the next unit, assuming that students "blew off" the test.

But these solutions do not address the issue of student learning. If students seemed to get it during formative assessments, then you should look at the test itself:

- How well do the items align with the concepts and processes in the unit's learning goals? Are you evaluating what you value? If you used a test from a previous year or one from the textbook, you might have to modify the number and types of questions if you emphasize different topics, expand on a topic based on student interest or needs, or cut some topics short based on the curriculum or lack of time.
- Are any items ambiguous or confusing, especially from the students' perspectives? Ask the students if they can explain their incorrect responses. This can help you identify poorly written items or those that used unfamiliar words. Perhaps the students still have misconceptions or were confused when they attempted to apply what they know to a new situation. Revise these questions.

Regardless of the reason for poor results, you should establish a policy on test retakes. You may give a similar test to the entire class, to selected students who performed poorly, or to any students who want to improve their scores. The focus of your retake policy should be on providing students with an opportunity to demonstrate their learning, although you'll have to establish a fair and consistent approach for assigning a grade to retakes.

Do your students know *how* to study for a test? We often have faulty assumptions, especially at the secondary level, that students have a wide range of study skills and know how and when to use them. You may need to guide students through note-taking and review processes. Fine-tune the generic study skills students were exposed to in previous years—skimming, summarizing, questioning, note-taking, highlighting—for your subject or grade level.

One of my favorite strategies is to ask the students, "What did you learn in this unit that I forgot to ask on the test?" It's interesting to see what students found memorable or relevant.

—Dwayne, grade 9 science teacher

Student Self-Assessment

How can I help my students with self-assessments?

Sherrie

Self-assessment is more than students checking off which answers they had wrong on their own papers. When students engage in self-assessment, they reflect on the results of their efforts and their progress toward meeting the learning goals. They look at their own work for evidence of quality, using established criteria on the rubrics. Based on their reflections, they can set personal learning goals and can begin to develop as independent learners.

Students don't necessarily come to your class with this skill, especially if their previous experiences have been in teacher-centered environments. They may need to be taught the strategies through examples and modeling. Students may initially think that an assignment (such as a lab report or project) is good simply because they spent a lot of time on it, enjoyed it, or worked very hard on it. Take a piece of student work (with no name on it) and guide students through the process of comparing the work to the rubric. You may have to do this several times before students feel comfortable critiquing their own work.

There are many types of activities that can be used as self-assessment strategies. Some of these are also formative assessment strategies, but in this case students are using them to monitor their own progress:

- In the "Learn" part of a KWL chart (see the "Preassessment" section of this chapter), students note what they are learning during the unit. Rather than writing a list of topics or vocabulary, students can use this as a form of self-assessment, responding to prompts such as the following:
    - I learned that …
    - I learned how to …
    - I need to learn more about …
- At the beginning of the unit, give each student a copy of the learning goals and a list of ways they can demonstrate their learning of each. Show students how to monitor their progress by checking off the goals as they are met.
- Using thumbs up or thumbs down and exit tickets, students express the status of their learning and indicate topics on which they are still confused.
- Student reflections are often included in science notebooks. Your modeling and guidance is important. Show students how you would reflect on your own learning.
- For projects, give each student a copy of the rubric when the assignment is given. Ask them to fill it out and submit it with the project. There could also be a place on the rubric for students to reflect on their projects:
    - This is a quality project because …

- o From doing this project I learned …
- o To make this project better, I could …
- o Our study team could have improved our work by …
- On tests, encourage students to mark the questions they didn't understand or had difficulty answering. This may also help you determine which test items to review or revise.

Honest self-assessment and reflection are difficult processes, even for adults. But it is a valuable tool for developing lifelong learners—we don't always have someone else to evaluate what we do.

Indicating Level of Success

What components should I consider when indicating level of success?

Jason

A final evaluation in the form of a student's grade should reflect the extent to which he or she has met the learning goals throughout the marking period.

Schools have different grading systems. Some use holistic A-B-C-D-F (or a 4-3-2-1 equivalent), some report percentages, and some use a standards-based system that reports student proficiency on the learning goals of the course. Consult with your mentor or department chair to learn about the system used in your school and how teachers assign grades. Before you establish your system for keeping records, be sure to look at the reporting system (progress reports) used by your school. It will have an effect on how you assess students and record the information you gather about each student.

Most teachers have a lot of leeway determining student grades. Here are some questions to consider:

- Should missing assignments be treated the same as cases where students did the work but demonstrated incomplete knowledge or misunderstandings?
- Should student absenteeism or behavior be factored into a grade?
- What will you do when students ask for extra credit work?
- Should practice exercises be factored into the grade?
- How will you record the information: letter grade, number, percentage, other?

It is very important that your grading reflects

- consistency,
- fairness, and
- informative input to students and parents.

> It's not a good idea to have students grade each other's work. But in a cooperative learning project, it can be helpful for students to provide feedback to each other prior to your looking at it.
>
> —Dale, grade 3 teacher

> I try to provide a variety of opportunities for students to show what they know and can do before assigning a final grade.
>
> —Joclyn, grade 7 science teacher

Conclusion

Statewide science assessments get a lot of publicity. These standardized assessments can be a part of an overall assessment plan. But it's important to understand that assessing student learning requires a variety of tools that can be adapted for different topics, different levels of learning goals, and different students. Adding tools to your toolkit is part of professional development.

Resources *(www.nsta.org/riseandshine)*

Assessments

Miami Museum of Science. Forms of Alternative Assessment: *www.miamisci.org/ph/lpdefine.html#AA*

SciLinks (keyword: Assessment): *www.scilinks.org*

Feedback

Brookhart, S. 2008. *How to give effective feedback to your students.* Alexandria, VA: Association for Supervision and Curriculum Development.

Wilson, M. B. 2011. Goodbye to "Good job!"—The power of specific feedback. *ASCD Express* 6: 10. *www.ascd.org/ascd-express/vol6/610-wilson.aspx?utm_source=ascdexpress&utm_medium=email&utm_campaign=express610*

Formative Assessments

Abell, S. K., and M. J. Volkmann. 2006. *Seamless assessment in science: A guide for elementary and middle school teachers.* Arlington, VA: NSTA Press.

Atkin, J. M., and J. E. Coffey. 2003. *Everyday assessment in the science classroom.* Arlington, VA: NSTA Press.

Brookhart, S. M. 2010. *How to assess higher-order thinking skills in your classroom.* Alexandria, VA: Association for Supervision and Curriculum Development.

Fisher, C., and N. Frey. 2007. *Checking for understanding: Formative assessment techniques for your classroom.* Alexandria, VA: Association for Supervision and Curriculum Development.

Keeley, P., et al. *Uncovering student ideas in science.* Arlington, VA: NSTA Press. (Series of books that contain formative assessment probes)

Marzano, R. 2010. *Formative assessment and standards-based grading.* Bloomington, IN: Marzano Research Laboratory.

Popham, E. J. 2008. *Transformative assessment.* Alexandria, VA: Association for Supervision and Curriculum Development.

KWL Charts

Hershberger, K., C. Zembal-Saul, and M. L. Starr. 2006. Evidence helps the KWL get a KLEW. *NSTA WebNews Digest. www.nsta.org/publications/news/story.aspx?id=51519&print=true*

Instructional Reading Strategy: KWL (Know, Want to Know, Learned): *www.indiana.edu/~l517/KWL.htm*

K-W-H-L Chart: *www.ncsu.edu/midlink/KWL.chart.html*

K-W-L Chart: *www.readwritethink.org/classroom-resources/printouts/chart-a-30226. html*

Using KWL to Introduce Inquiry: *www.exploratorium.edu/IFI/resources/ lifescienceinquiry/usingkwl.html*

Rubrics

Assessment and Rubric Information: *http://school.discoveryeducation.com/ schrockguide/edref.html*

Assessment Rubrics: *http://edtech.kennesaw.edu/intech/rubrics.htm*

iRubric: *www.iRubric.com*

Lantz, H. B. 2004. Rubrics for assessing student achievement in science grades K–12. Thousand Oaks, CA: Corwin Press.

Rubrics: *http://jfmueller.faculty.noctrl.edu/toolbox/rubrics.htm*

Rubrics for Assessment: *www.uwstout.edu/soe/profdev/rubrics.shtml*

RubiStar: *http://rubistar.4teachers.org/index.php*

Tech for Learning: *http://myt4l.com/index.php?v=pl&page_ac=view&type=tools &tool=rubricmaker*

Test Banks and Released Items

AAAS Project 2061 Science Assessment: *http://assessment.aaas.org*

MOSART (Misconceptions-Oriented Standards-Based Assessment Resources for Teachers): *www.cfa.harvard.edu/smgphp/mosart/*

NAEP Science Assessment: *www.nationsreportcard.gov/science_2009/sample_quest. asp?tab_id=tab2&subtab_id=Tab_1*

PALS (Performance Assessment Links in Science): *http://pals.sri.com*

Released State Tests and Sample Tests: *www.edinformatics.com/testing*

TIMSS Assessment Questions (Grades 4 and 8): *http://nces.ed.gov/timss/ educators.asp*

Online Appendixes

8.1 Teacher Suggestions for Grading Papers

8.2a KWL Chart

8.2b Unit KWL Chart

8.2c Types of Rocks Unit KWL Chart

CHAPTER 9
CREATING PROFESSIONAL DEVELOPMENT OPPORTUNITIES

Dear Ms. Mentor,

Alberto

I'm changing to a middle school teaching position. My specialty is biology, but now I'm teaching environmental science. The inservice agenda for this year focuses on teaching strategies, but what I really need are crash courses in the content. I can't go back to college—what can I do?

Dear Alberto,

Science teachers have two fields requiring continuing education—pedagogy and science content. It's easy for a school to plan professional development in teaching practices. Topics such as cooperative learning, classroom management, technology, curriculum design, inclusion, and assessment apply to virtually all subject areas. But science content is another issue. For a small group of science teachers, it's difficult (and costly) to find facilitators to provide workshops or seminars on specific science topics. A popular solution is to combine with teachers from other schools for the traditional "large group in an auditorium for a speaker" event. However, these one-shot presentations without any follow-up can be ineffective.

Many of our students have IEPs (Individualized Education Plans) to meet their needs. Perhaps it's time for teachers to create IPDPs (Individualized Professional Development Plans), particularly for content knowledge. Some states and districts offer such an option for self-directed learning. Teachers set their own learning goals, design learning activities, document their activities, and describe how they will apply the new content knowledge. The plans require prior approval (especially if the district is awarding official professional development hours) and usually teachers are excused from some or all of the traditional inservice programs. Perhaps you could offer to pilot an IPDP in your school.

Keep your plan simple and doable. Identify one or two content topics to start, perhaps the ones in which you feel least confident. It sounds like you have goals (updating your content knowledge and skills and finding related resources and activities for your classroom).

Not all content learning activities have to be in a formal graduate course. Consider activities such as reading science journals or trade books (check out the suggested reading lists in the NSTA journals), viewing videos and television programs related to science, listening to podcasts, reading relevant websites or blogs, or participating in a professional learning community (including online communities). Look for seminars or speakers at nearby colleges and universities or professional societies. Consider visiting a science museum, zoo, planetarium, nature center, or botanical garden that offers programs compatible with your goals. Reading articles from NSTA journals such as *The Science Teacher, Science Scope,* and *Science & Children* is an easy way to stay current on both pedagogy and content.

Keep a record of your learning in a journal, on your computer, or on a form supplied by your school as documentation. The NSTA Learning Center has a PD Plan and Portfolio tool to guide you through designing a plan. Other Learning Center resources include self-directed learning modules, webinars, podcasts, discussion groups, and Listservs. You may be surprised at how informal professional learning can add to your content knowledge base.

—Ms. Mentor

ALONG WITH THE materials you received during your orientation, you probably received a list of dates for inservice days. These days are part of your teaching contract, and they can be used for a variety of activities. Some might be work days to get your classroom ready or to grade exams. Some days may be set aside for meetings, and others may be designated for professional development.

Heather — *What happens on an inservice day?*

Some professional development is in the form of training that is important to everyone in the system. If the school is implementing new software for attendance, grading, or communications, then it's essential that all teachers and staff get the necessary training and subsequent updates. Other types of PD should address the needs of individuals.

Researchers are studying what constitutes successful, individualized professional development for educators in an effort to improve teaching. Some have found that observing other teachers in the classroom (or watching videos of classrooms) and providing feedback for teachers is effective. However, the professional development that teachers need might differ based on their content area. For example, science teachers say their training should be more content-specific. It may be that you will be required to formulate or find your own professional development opportunities in the content areas. Your school system may provide professional development for pedagogy but likely will not for science content.

> I would hesitate to use an accountant who last attended a tax seminar in 1995 or a doctor who never went to seminars to learn about new medical procedures. Teachers, as professionals, have the obligation to maintain and update their skills and knowledge base.
>
> —Ty, middle school principal

Developing a Plan

Sherrie — *How do I begin developing a plan for my professional development?*

Even if your school does not require one, it's important for you to have your own plan for continuing education. You can begin by generating a list of what you want to learn. Perhaps it is science-related content, or maybe it's a teaching strategy you want to learn more about (→ see Chapter 7, "Teaching Strategies"). You can easily identify these areas by keeping an ongoing list of ideas, beginning on the first day of school. Prioritize the topics and consider what amount of time you have available to dedicate to this new learning. Design a plan that will guide your learning:

- Select one topic that you have found to be of greatest interest. It's practical to begin with one that supports you in your current role—a skill or topic you can use immediately.
- Identify a goal or need related to the topic. What is it about this topic that will help you be a better teacher? For example, you may identify a need to learn more about how to use cooperative learning in a lab setting

> If you are choosing graduate courses, think of an overall plan that may lead to a degree or another certification rather than taking a hodgepodge of courses.
>
> —Shayna, special education teacher

> While attending a leadership seminar, one of the presenters shared some interesting research. She stated the following:
>
> • 87% of people don't have goals.
> • 10% of people have goals but don't write them down.
> • 3% of people have written goals.
>
> The 3% accomplish 50 to 100 times more of their goals than others.
>
> —Lisa, high school principal

> When I was a new teacher, several of us started an informal book discussion group. In addition to the reading, it was a time for us to socialize and learn from each other's experiences.
>
> —Joclyn, grade 7 science teacher

or to incorporate more inquiry into your labs, or you may have gaps in your content knowledge.

- Identify possible avenues to take to accomplish your goal (there may be several). Some will be easily accomplished through personal reading, observing in another classroom, taking a class at a nearby university, participating in science conferences, collaborating with others via social media, enrolling in workshops provided by informal science centers, or finding information online.
- Create a timeline indicating key dates for the activities.
- Decide on how you'll know when you've met your goal (you may need to revisit it if you aren't satisfied with the results). Don't hesitate to revise it as the year progresses.
- There are online PD planners that will assist you in focusing on your needs. (→ See Online Appendix 9.1, "Sample Teacher's Professional Development Portfolio," and Chapter 13 for more on professional activities.)

An easy way to begin your personal professional development is through reflecting on your teaching. You can do this alone and you can do it on the spot. Simply think about what occurred in class during the day. Jot notes as to what you might have done to improve student learning. Consider what you can do the next day to follow up on the development of student understanding.

Book Groups

A professional book group is one of the most convenient and readily applicable professional development opportunities to design because it allows you to select the date, time, and topic of your study.

Some groups read an entire book and then discuss sections of it, while other groups work through books together. You will find that many books are created with book groups in mind. You'll find that some contain chunks of information that are appropriate for the group to read and study together as well as providing discussion questions and implementation assignments. (→ See Online Appendix 9.2 for ideas on setting up a book group.)

Professional Associations

I am not a member of any professional associations. There are so many of them. How do I know which ones to join?

Heather

Professional organizations can provide you with many valuable learning experiences and there are many from which to choose. Memberships can be costly, particularly on a new teacher's salary, so careful selection is important. The offerings vary, but most have now gone to web-based support for your PD needs, which makes your search easier. Obviously, if you are a biology teacher, you might not be interested in an association geared toward physics instruction. But don't rule it out quite yet. (→ See the Resources list or Online Appendix 11.1 for a list of organizations.)

Consider your needs and the goals of your PD plan. Are you seeking more content knowledge? Help in creating curriculum? Strategies to use immediately in your classroom? Suggestions for working with a particular student population (e.g., early childhood, special needs, urban, rural)? Begin with a list of organizations and explore some of the options. If you don't find what you need, try a web search. Here are some steps you can take to determine which associations are a good fit for you:

- ❏ Be specific rather than broad. Let's use Earth science as an example. If you Google *Earth science teaching associations*, you will find several national associations (National Science Teachers Association [NSTA], National Earth Science Teachers Association [NESTA], and Earth Science Teachers Association [UK]), as well as state associations.
- ❏ Go to the site of the association and look at what they have to offer. Most have journals or newsletters. Do those documents provide you with what you are seeking? Do they have a conference, publications, web tools that support learning, and other benefits?
- ❏ Now consider broadening your search. You may find that larger, all-encompassing associations can provide you with more resources for your dollar. If you enter *science teaching associations* in a search engine, you will once again find national associations (NSTA, National Association for Research in Science Teaching [NARST], NESTA) and state associations.
- ❏ Broaden your search one more time. A web search for *science associations* will reveal several national associations, including the American Association for the Advancement of Science (AAAS).

You can repeat this search strategy for any topic. Consider curriculum development, educational leadership, educational supervision, or professional development associations, to name a few.

> Many professional associations offer reduced dues and special resources for new teachers.
>
> —Dwayne, grade 9 science teacher

Conference Participation

My mentor wants me to attend a nearby conference with her. What goes on at a conference? How should I prepare?

Jason

Participation in a conference is one of the best ways to quickly gather content, pedagogy, materials, and equipment information. Nearly everything you are seeking will be in one location, and you will find many options for professional development. You'll find large-group sessions featuring prominent science researchers; small-group sessions (often presented by teachers) that focus on specific topics or learning strategies; and an exhibit area with booths set up by vendors of science lab equipment, textbooks, professional science organizations, and agencies such as NASA or NOAA. Veteran conference-goers agree that face-to-face networking among teachers is another valuable component. Check with your department chair concerning what the school system requires for your attendance. There are a few essential steps you should follow to be prepared:

> About the time I feel as if burnout is setting in, it's time to attend the national NSTA conference. Each time I attend, I return to my students invigorated and eager to try all of the new ideas I have learned. Good-bye, burnout.
>
> —Sharon, grade 5 teacher

☐ Identify a conference you are interested in attending. This should be done well in advance.

☐ Begin to plan. Once you have received approval to attend, begin to finalize your plans. Make lists of topics of interest as well as materials that you hope to better understand.

☐ Create a personal schedule. Most large conferences have a website dedicated to the event. Be sure to reserve time to visit the exhibit floor. Once you have a plan in place, ask your department chair or mentor to look it over and give you input concerning your selections.

☐ Have your schedule and support items in hand at the conference. Divide and conquer if you're attending with a friend or colleague, going your separate ways and then sharing what you've learned when you meet up again. Keep a log or journal of the sessions you attended, people you met, and new ideas you've learned. Update your home page, Facebook, or class wiki or blog with a summary of what you are learning at the conference. Create a transcript of everything you attend.

☐ Follow-up is important. After the conference, it's wise to let your administrator know how you are using your newly gained knowledge as you implement what you have learned.

The list above provides a brief overview (→ see Online Appendix 9.3 for a conference participation checklist).

Professional Learning Communities

Teachers in your school may be involved in learning together as a community. Some of these groups are informal and meet based on the interests of small groups. Others involve the entire school. Formal professional learning communities (PLCs) may be something unfamiliar to many educators, although they are gaining attention. PLCs are based on the idea that schools should be learning places for both children and adults. The basic understanding is that one important key to improved learning is continuous job-embedded learning for educators. In its standards, the National Staff Development Council recognizes PLCs as a strategy for school improvement—specifically, as a way to support high-quality and ongoing professional development. There are two basic assumptions surrounding the construction and implementation of professional development in a PLC:

- Knowledge is situated in the day-to-day experiences of teachers and is best understood through critical reflection with others who share the same experiences.
- Actively engaging teachers in PLCs will increase their professional knowledge and enhance student learning.

PLCs are characterized by several traits that are supported by the shared values and vision held by the entire school community. This is a major commitment by a school, and a great deal of research should be conducted to gain a full understanding of the implications of becoming involved in a PLC. (→ See Resources for more about PLCs.) Some of the characteristics of PLCs are as follows:

- *Collaborative culture:* PLCs are based on collaboration—professionals who learn together achieve more than they could alone. Teachers benefit from the resources that each brings to the PLC. Collaboration provides a mechanism for sharing responsibility for student learning and a way to work together toward a common purpose. Collaboration provides opportunities for teachers to engage in ongoing collegial interaction where they talk about teaching, receive frequent feedback on teaching, design classes together, and teach each other.

- *Focus on examining outcomes to improve student learning:* PLCs promote results-oriented thinking that is focused on continuous improvement and student learning. The focus goes beyond a team getting together to look at data. In PLCs, teachers respond to data that require accountability and changing classroom practices. Data help motivate teachers to see what is happening and what they need to do collectively.

- *Supportive and shared leadership:* PLCs often are viewed as a foundation for developing teacher leaders. Administrators are committed to sharing decision making with teachers and providing them with leadership opportunities. Leadership is shared and distributed among formal and informal leaders.

- *Shared personal practice:* A major focus of PLCs is on professional learning in which teachers work and learn together as they continually evaluate the effectiveness of their practices and the needs, interests, and skills of their students. Teachers share experiences, observe each other, and discuss teaching. Shared practice and collective inquiry help sustain improvement by strengthening connections among teachers, stimulating discussion about professional practice, and helping teachers build on one another's expertise. Through continuous inquiry and reflective dialogue, teachers discover solutions and address student needs.

> Even experienced teachers find working in PLCs to be a lot of work, but worth it!
>
> —Ty, middle school principal

Using Community Resources

One of the easiest ways to create a professional development opportunity is to work with your local university. (If you don't have one close by, consider the next topic in our discussion, e-learning.)

Tanya

I have been going to school nearly all of my life. I want a break from that. What else can I do to increase my expertise without going back to college?

- Although the first idea you might have is that you should go to campus and take a course, perhaps you do not want to go back to school quite yet, especially if you are a recent graduate. Universities have many other opportunities available. Consider their lecture series, workshops, and other special events.

- If you find a large group of colleagues who are interested in the same course, consider inviting the university to come to you. Many universities offer satellite courses. They are taught in schools by university faculty. This allows you the convenience of not leaving the building to participate in a class, and you have the advantage of working with a group of teachers who will all participate in the same learning activities. You and your colleagues can gain a lot from such an experience when you begin to implement what you have learned.

- Once you have been in the classroom for a few years, you may want to consider becoming a cooperating teacher. This provides an opportunity for student teachers to come into your room and learn from you. Anyone who has ever done this will probably tell you that they learn as much from the preservice teacher as the new professional learns from them.

Research other local opportunities. You may find that informal science centers (science museums, zoos, nature centers) offer workshops and summer institutes. This frequently includes opportunities to earn continuing education units that are accepted by your school system. These science centers may also provide volunteer docent opportunities and resources for classroom use.

E-Learning

More than 75% of colleges and universities in the United States offer online degree programs, with online degrees as respected as "on the ground" degrees. Many professional associations offer online learning opportunities as well. There are several benefits to online instruction, videoconferencing, and other forms of distance learning.

Alberto

How can I locate e-learning opportunities?

- You can attend a course anytime, from anywhere.
- In many cases, course material is accessible 24 hours per day, 7 days per week.
- Online instructors come with practical knowledge and may be from any location across the globe. This allows students to be exposed to knowledge that can't be learned in books, as well as allowing them to see how class concepts are applied to real situations.
- Participating online may be much less intimidating than participating in the classroom.
- Many online institutions offer chat rooms for informal conversation between students.
- The online environment makes instructors more approachable. Students can talk openly with their teachers through online chats, e-mail, and newsgroup discussions without waiting for office hours that may be inconvenient.
- Online course development allows for a broad spectrum of content. Many institutions allow access to the school's library for those participating in online learning.
- Online classrooms also facilitate team learning by providing chat rooms and newsgroups for meetings and joint work. This eliminates the problems of having mismatched schedules, finding a meeting location, and distributing work for review between meetings.

Before you select an e-learning experience, there are several factors you should consider.

- Do you (or your school system) have access to the equipment necessary to participate in this type of learning? Different sites require different technology, so be sure you have access to what you'll need.
- Is the course synchronous or asynchronous? In a synchronous course, there are specific times you are required to log in and participate in a live presentation or discussion. In an asynchronous course, you can access the materials anytime. Some courses use a combination of these formats.
- Do you have information concerning the leader for this experience? Is the experience sponsored by an organization that has a reputation for providing quality resources?
- What expenses are associated with the experience? Will you need to meet face-to-face at any time, which might require travel? Many universities offer free online learning (e.g., Carnegie Mellon University;

Don't sign up for an e-learning experience thinking it will be an easy course requiring little time. I have found them to be rigorous and as engaging as any classroom experience.

—Lisa, high school principal

Massachusetts Institute of Technology (MIT); University of California, Berkeley; Tufts University; Open University). A great website that identifies many universities is eLearning.com, or you can search for science distance learning.

- If you are attempting to earn professional development or continuing education units for this experience, is this site recognized as a provider? If it's a graduate program, is it accredited, and do both your school and the state accreditation office accept the credits or recognize the degree?
- What type of work is expected of you beyond participation in the online events or videoconferences?
- As with all PD, consider what you must bring to the experience during each session. Do you have the time necessary to complete all of the work required?
- A major consideration is the time you have available to dedicate to this commitment. Be cautious in overcommitting yourself, especially during the first couple of years of teaching. Right now, your teaching assignment should take priority over the commitment of further course work.

E-learning is not limited to formal classes. Most teachers, even those who are seasoned veterans of the profession, find that e-connecting through Listservs, Twitter, Facebook, and other communities and social networking sites provides valuable learning experiences through sharing.

E-learning has limitations. Some argue there is a disadvantage in not being with others who are participating—the collegial aspect. One way to avoid this obstacle is to invite others on your team to participate with you. Create your own learning environment and support one another as you learn. The opportunity to participate in professional development that goes beyond what is available locally may be well worth inconveniences and limitations.

Professional Networking

Part of being a member of a profession is that professionals provide help to one another. Most teachers don't consider this as being available to them. Many even say, "I just shut my door and teach." Your network can be an important professional development support group—not to mention the support other teachers can provide that falls outside the academic realm.

Take advantage of social media, such as Facebook or Twitter, and the Listservs and discussion forums that many organizations have available. These are wonderful opportunities for just-in-time ideas or discussing topics in depth.

Every teacher you meet has the potential to provide you with support, if not now, then perhaps in the future. No matter how strong you believe your memory is, you will not recall information about the many people you meet. Keep track on an electronic device or in a journal or notepad specifically for this purpose. Include the teacher's name, where he works, contact information, and how he is connected to education (and you).

> You don't need to go very far to participate in excellent professional development. Don't underestimate the value of observing one of your colleagues. A lot can be gained from observing a fellow teacher, especially a great one.
>
> —Richard, science department chair

It is impossible to predict how people might be important to you in the future. Perhaps you will seek a new job, consider a move to another location, or prepare a manuscript based on something in which they have expertise. Return the favor. It is important to reciprocate with support to other professionals when requested.

Conclusion

Most school mission statements include the goal of lifelong learning for the students. When teachers are also lifelong learners, it sends a powerful message to students. Begin your selection of future professional development activities by preparing a list of possible topics. As you read articles, teach content, and confront issues and obstacles, add topics to your list. You will find this helpful in the future when you make final selections and request time and resources from your supervisor.

Resources *(www.nsta.org/riseandshine)*

Professional Learning Communities

DuFour, R., and R. Eaker. 1998. *Professional learning communities at work: Best practices for enhancing student achievement.* Alexandria, VA: Association for Supervision and Curriculum Development.

Mundry, S., and K. E. Stiles. 2009. *Professional learning communities for science teaching: Lessons from research and practice.* Arlington, VA: NSTA Press.

Southwest Educational Development Laboratory (SEDL). 1997. Professional learning communities: What they are and why they are important. *Issues ... About Change* 6 (1). *www.sedl.org/change/issues/issues61.html*

Subject-Specific Organizations for Science Teachers

American Association of Physics Teachers (AAPT): *www.aapt.org*

American Chemical Society (ACS; Division of Chemical Education): *http://portal.acs.org/portal/acs/corg/content*

National Association of Biology Teachers (NABT): *www.nabt.org/websites/institution/index.php?p=1*

National Earth Science Teachers Association (NESTA): *www.nestanet.org*

National Marine Educators Association (NMEA): *www.marine-ed.org*

National Middle Level Science Teachers Association (NMLSTA): *www.nmlsta.org*

Organizations Related to Science Education

American Association for the Advancement of Science (AAAS): *www.aaas.org*

Association for Multicultural Science Education (AMSE): *www.amsek16.org/www.amsek16.org/Welcome.html*

Association of Science-Technology Centers (ASTC): *www.astc.org*

Association for Science Teacher Education (ASTE): *http://theaste.org*

Council for Elementary Science International (CESI): *www.cesiscience.org*

International Council of Associations for Science Education (ICASE): *www.icaseonline.net*

National Academy of Sciences (NAS): *www.nasonline.org*

National Association for Research in Science Teaching (NARST): *www.narst.org*
National Institute for Science Education (NISE): *http://archive.wceruw.org/nise*
National Science Education Leadership Association (NSELA): *www.nsela.org*
National Science Foundation (NSF): *www.nsf.gov*
National Science Teachers Association (NSTA): *www.nsta.org*
School Science and Mathematics Association (SSMA): *www.ssma.org*

Other Educational Organizations

Association for Middle Level Education (AMLE; formerly National Middle School Association): *www.amle.org*
Association for Supervision and Curriculum Development (ASCD): *www.ascd.org*
International Reading Association (IRA): *www.reading.org*
International Society for Technology in Education (ISTE): *www.iste.org*
National Association of Elementary School Principals (NAESP): *www.naesp.org*
National Association of Secondary School Principals (NASSP): *www.nassp.org*
National Council of Teachers of Mathematics (NCTM): *www.nctm.org*
Phi Delta Kappa: *www.pdkintl.org*

Online Appendixes

9.1 Sample Teacher's Professional Development Portfolio
9.2 How to Set Up a Professional Book Group
9.3 Conference Participation Checklist

CHAPTER 10
PARENTS AS PARTNERS

Dear Ms. Mentor,

Jason

My school wants to encourage more parental involvement. Any suggestions?

Dear Jason,

Parental involvement is a term we *think* we all understand, but it might help to discuss what "involved" parents look like. Are they the parents or caregivers who come to open houses or conferences, belong to the parent-teacher organization, attend school events, call with questions about their child's learning, and make sure their child does homework? Are they the parents who do the homework for the child, question you repeatedly about grading, second-guess your instructional decisions or school policy, make unreasonable demands on your time, or assume their child is always correct?

And what about the parents who work multiple jobs to pay bills, have difficulty communicating in English, are experiencing their own personal or medical problems, or stay away because of negative experiences they had when they were students?

I prefer the term *parental support* to describe what parents can do to be a part of their child's education. Surprisingly, some parents may not know how to be supportive. Communication and positive experiences with schools can be the first steps in promoting parent support.

If we communicate only negative information (behavior issues, low test scores, missing homework), it's understandable why parents and caregivers might not want much contact. A high school I worked in had a "Good News" project. Teachers were encouraged to send postcards (provided by the school) to parents to share positive student events: an improved grade, helpful behaviors, or an interesting activity. The school secretary would address and mail them (e-mail works too). Many parents would call to thank us for the good news.

RISE AND SHINE: A Practical Guide for the Beginning Science Teacher

Parents also should be able to find information easily on the school's website. Class web pages or blogs could describe activities, assignments, and deadlines. Some schools add a twist to the traditional school calendar. In addition to sporting events and holidays, every week has suggestions for a simple activity parents could do with their children. The calendar also has information about the local public library and nearby museums. Some schools have take-home packs that include books, science mini-kits, or puzzles and games.

It may be hard to believe, but many parents get nervous when they have to visit their child's school. Nonthreatening, pleasant experiences can help them overcome their anxiety. A middle school switched from a teacher-centered back-to-school night to an open house concept, encouraging students and other family members to come along. The students introduced their parents and teachers, gave their families a tour of the lab, and showed them their lab notebooks. If parents wanted to talk about their child in detail, they left their names and the teacher contacted them.

Some schools are including students in the parent conferences so students can share their work and be part of the discussion.

We can wait for external solutions to what we perceive as a lack of parent involvement or support, or we can communicate with parents and caregivers, provide nonthreatening opportunities for them to visit the school, and help them learn how to be supportive.

—Ms. Mentor

THE WORD *PARENT* is used throughout this chapter, but be aware that other adults may play important roles in your students' lives: guardians, stepparents, grandparents or other relatives, foster parents, and other caregivers. When you use the word *parent*, you should consider all of these possibilities.

Although teachers have a huge influence on students, no one can have the effect on students that parents can. No matter the student's age, the approval of parents is a fundamental need of every child and a powerful motivator. Parents can support you in providing time for one-to-one academic help as well as discipline follow-through.

Contacting Parents

Heather

What should I do to make initial contact with parents? What kind of information should I share?

Contacting parents early and often is key to developing a positive working relationship. It's never too early in the year to let them know that you are aware of their child's strengths and weaknesses and that you care about their student's success. Some teachers initiate contact before school begins with a simple welcome note or phone call. Early in the year, contact parents with good news. Genuine caring can be shown when you contact parents when their child has done something positive—from social interactions to academic successes. If you wait to contact a parent with negative news, you have not had the opportunity to develop a working relationship based on their child's positive attributes.

A good guide to follow is to think about the type of communication you would like to have if your child were in the class. In other words, put yourself in the shoes of the parent. Ask yourself these questions:

- ❏ What kind of information do I want concerning the curriculum?
- ❏ When and how often would I like to speak with the teacher?
- ❏ How do I want the teacher to communicate with me?
- ❏ What kind of information do I want concerning the social interactions my child is having in the classroom?
- ❏ What kind of information do I need to support my child in being successful?
- ❏ How would I like to respond to the communication?

Be deliberate and don't just let parent communication happen on its own. Communicating with parents requires a plan that includes working with them all year long. Take a proactive attitude. Know when, where, and how you will contact parents—develop a plan for parent involvement. That plan will require organization and record-keeping. But remember, if you let communication just happen, it may likely be a negative experience. Don't wait for parents to contact you. Don't let a problem be the reason for the first communication you have with parents.

Provide an opportunity for parents to get to know you; do this before the end of the first week of school. Send home a note telling them about yourself and your goals for the school year. Include information on lab safety (→ see Chapter 5 for more information on safety contracts and student orientation). The tone should be upbeat and show your eagerness to have a wonderful school year. Tell parents that students need their support to be successful this year. End the letter with a positive message exhibiting confidence in the success you anticipate. Tell them about future correspondence plans and your course syllabus. You may also want

> Communicating with parents is often simply a matter of common sense. Tell them what is going on in your classroom and why. Treat them the way you would like to be treated as a parent.
>
> —Dale, grade 3 teacher

to tell them how they can contact you, including times you are available to take phone calls and the time of day you typically respond to e-mail.

Conferences

Verbal communication can be in the form of a telephone conference or a face-to-face meeting. Consider the topic and type of experience you want to create in determining which type of discussion you will have with a parent. Due to your schedule and that of the parents, a phone call might be the best avenue. If it is a quick check-in to share a piece of information or provide positive input, the phone is a great way to accomplish your goals. Although it may seem that an e-mail may be the best way to communicate, consider the fact that an e-mail cannot as clearly express your enthusiasm, empathy, concern, or joy as well as your own voice.

Phone Conferences

All communications with parents should be entered into a log. The log should indicate attempts you have made to contact parents as well as discussions you have had. If you script your phone calls, include that in the record. If you have sent an e-mail, print out your comments and their responses. A three-ring binder with a log page for each student is a good way to maintain this record because it will allow you to include notes, student work, safety contracts, and anecdotal records as reminders of past communications. Some electronic grading systems also have a place to record notes for each student.

Before you make a phone call carefully consider what you are going to say. You may even want to create a script or checklist, especially for your first few telephone conferences. You might also want to invite your mentor to listen to the call and then provide you with input. Some of the suggested comments to include are listed below:

Tanya: I know that phone conferences are an appropriate way to communicate. How do I begin the conversation and what should I say?

- ☐ Introduce yourself not only by name but also by the role you play in the life of their child.
- ☐ Begin with the reason for your call. Present it with an appropriate tone of voice and express concern or joy. This will set the tone of the entire conversation.
- ☐ In the case of calls regarding concerns, the next steps should involve the following:
    - ○ Be specific and give examples of the behavior or occurrence that concerns you.
    - ○ Describe steps you have taken to solve the problem.

- ○ Ask if the parents have had experience in the past with a similar concern. Get their input regarding their point of view.
- ○ Ask for their suggestions as to what they consider necessary to providing a successful school experience for their child.
- ○ Discuss what you will do together to provide the support this child needs to be successful.
- ○ Plan for follow-up communication in regard to your concern and the success of the student.
- ❏ No matter the type of call, end it in a positive manner. Be optimistic about the success you know the student is capable of achieving. Be sensitive to the needs of the parent and child.

A follow-up phone call should occur at the time you have agreed to during the initial call. Be sure to include the following information:

- ❏ What the student has done to correct the issue
- ❏ The progress the student has made
- ❏ How the parent's cooperation has been helpful
- ❏ What follow-up needs to occur, (schedule subsequent phone calls if needed)

(See "Dealing With Political and Volatile Agendas" [p. 142] for information concerning how to address individuals who may become belligerent or hostile.)

Face-to-Face Conferences

Sometimes it is desirable to meet with a parent in person. These conferences can happen before school, after school, during your planning period, or during class (someone will have to cover your class for you). These conferences take place in a conference room, the principal's office, or your classroom. The location should foster private conversation in nonthreatening surroundings.

> *Sherrie*
>
> *Planning for my first conference with parents is a little scary. I simply don't know all of the important details to consider in setting up the conference and carrying it through. Where do I begin?*

> Never lose sight that you and the parents are working together to support this child both socially and academically—you are partners.
>
> —Shayna, special education teacher

Plan the conference and be sure everything you need for successful communication is available. Determine who should be in attendance. In addition to you and the parent, should the teaching team and/or the student be involved? If a team is involved, have a preconference planning session to determine one or two problems that will be discussed, coordinate documents that will be used, and list the specific points to be made. Select a facilitator for the conference who will lead the discussion. If you are conducting a conference on your own, carefully structure each detail:

- ☐ Schedule the conference with a time limit.
- ☐ Gather documentation to share with the parents. This can be anecdotal notes or student work.
- ☐ Write down all of the important points you want to make.
  - ○ Begin with your concern.
  - ○ Describe the specific concern and provide documentation.
  - ○ Explain what you have been doing to support the student.
  - ○ Get input from the parents concerning their past experiences and possible solutions.
  - ○ Determine what the parents will do to help, as well as what you will do.
  - ○ Express confidence that you and the parents can help support the student.
  - ○ Discuss follow-up. Determine if it will be another conference, a phone call, an e-mail, or a note. Set a specific date. Be sure to allow time for result of the efforts to be successful.
- ☐ Keep in mind how the parents will feel and create a positive atmosphere. Do not sit at your desk or have a barrier between you and the parents. Instead, sit side by side at a table. Create an atmosphere of collegiality. You are working together to help their child.
  - ○ Maintain eye contact.
  - ○ Maintain a body posture that shows openness and welcoming (no crossed arms).
  - ○ Lean toward the parents when they are speaking.
  - ○ Sit quietly when the parents are talking. Be an active, reflective listener.

(See "Dealing With Political and Volatile Agendas" [p. 142] for information concerning how to address individuals who may become belligerent or hostile.)

Back-to-School Night

Jason

The thought of back-to-school night is already making me nervous. What should I expect?

The back-to-school event may be the first time you meet your students' parents. This is the time to put your best foot forward and engage the parents in science. Plan ahead and create a feeling of organization and confidence. Select your attire

> Before any conference when there will be sharing of negative comments, I always remember that every student is worth my effort. Some students need my care and affection more when they seem to deserve it the least.
>
> —Dale, grade 3 teacher

to reflect the professional, confident image you want to convey. You may want to wear a lab coat (be sure it is clean) if that is what students generally see you wear.

Whether it's held before school starts or during the first few weeks, this annual event provides an opportunity for the important adults in a student's life to meet one another. It also gives parents or other caregivers a chance to become more familiar with the school. Ask a colleague what format is used in your school, what the expectations are, and how the event is publicized. Most schools have their event during the first month or so of the school year.

Typically, the parent is given a modified copy of the student's schedule to follow during a back-to-school night. The bell rings as parents move from classroom to classroom for brief periods. The schedule is very compact; there often is only time for brief introductions. There's not much time for questions and conversations or for parents to look around your classroom or lab before the next bell rings.

An open house is less structured. Parents get a copy of the student's schedule but are free to visit the classrooms in any order. This is a more leisurely pace, but you can be overwhelmed if you get a lot of parents at once or if one parent starts to monopolize your time.

With either format, some schools also invite students to attend as a "take your parents to school" event. This provides students with the opportunity to introduce their parents and teachers. Students can guide their parents to the classrooms and show them some of their work.

One of the first steps is to prepare your classroom. It should represent what occurs in your room and project a positive image:

- ❏ Prepare a sign-in sheet with spaces for the parent's name, the student's name, and a phone number or e-mail address you can use to contact the parent. Place this near the entry door.
- ❏ Be sure your room is easy to identify in the hallway. Make a sign with your name, room number, and class or subject clearly displayed.
- ❏ Create an exhibit of science equipment you will use throughout the year with labels.
- ❏ Be sure safety equipment and posters are clearly in view.
- ❏ Select examples of ungraded student-generated work to post in the room.
- ❏ Clean and tidy up the room (you may need to stow some items).
- ❏ Have textbooks or other print materials available for parents to preview.
- ❏ Post the class schedule.
- ❏ Post the curriculum topics you will study.

I would like to provide back-to-school night participants with a handout. What types of things should I consider including?

Alberto

You may want to consider providing handouts. They may include not only your classroom expectations but also the school expectations. Consider including the following:

- ❏ A single page with your philosophy and contact information (see Chapter 1 for more on developing your teaching philosophy)
- ❏ A syllabus or outline of your course describing what students will learn this year (→ see Online Appendix 3.1 for examples of course syllabi)
- ❏ Your lab safety contract (→ see Online Appendix 5.1 for a safety agreement from NSTA)
- ❏ Discipline policy
- ❏ Homework policy
- ❏ Absence/makeup work policy
- ❏ Parent handbook (usually provided through the front office)

Plan what you are going to say. You may want to prepare an outline or script your comments. This will give you more confidence as you face a room full of parents for the first time. As you speak, be sure to allow time for parents to ask questions. You can tell them that you will allow time at the end for questions, and if they have further questions they may call you.

- ❏ Introduce yourself by giving them a brief account of your background, where you went to school, your degree(s), prior experiences in education- and science-related fields, and a few words about your interests.
- ❏ Tell them you want to work with them as a team to provide the best learning experience for their children.
- ❏ Tell them about
  - ○ how you will communicate with them, when you check e-mail, when you return phone calls, and how they can get in touch with you;
  - ○ your philosophy;
  - ○ your discipline plan;
  - ○ the homework policy;
  - ○ makeup work;
  - ○ extra help;
  - ○ additional lab times;
  - ○ field trips and special events; and
  - ○ the curriculum, what their children will study, and special projects, such as a science fair.
- ❏ Ask for their help in supporting their children at home (→ see Online Appendix 7.6, "Student Guide for Learning"). Give parents tips on how they can help students at home. This can be done by making homework a priority, providing a quiet (distraction-free) place for them to study, specifying a time for studying, and providing positive

> If a parent asks a question that you have not had an opportunity to think about, take a deep breath. Think before speaking. If you have no response that allows you to fully explain the question, then tell them you will get back to them on the topic soon. Then set a date and get back to them.
>
> —Lisa, high school principal

reinforcement for completing work to the best of the child's ability.
(→ See Chapter 7 for more on homework.)

☐ Encourage parents to share their talents. Ask them to contact you if they are experts in any of the fields that will be studied during the year. Consider them for guest speaker roles, volunteers for field trips, outdoor fieldwork guides, or assistants for labs or investigations that require additional adults in the classroom.

☐ If you have time, engage parents in a demonstration or discrepant event. Select a quick activity that their students may be involved in sometime during the school year.

Plan your back-to-school night event as thoroughly as you would any lesson for your students. Greet parents at the door with a firm handshake and a smile. Listen to what parents have to say and follow up with anyone who seemed to exhibit concerns. Also, follow up with any parents who may not have attended by sending home your handouts and/or contacting them with an e-mail message concerning what was discussed at back-to-school night.

Comments on Report Cards

The use of computers has revolutionized the number and quality of comments that can be provided to parents. Some school systems provide a program that allows the selection of comments that can be included on the progress report. If you don't have this type of tool, you can create your own database of comments that can be pasted into a document. You'll then have ready-made topics and comments to share. Comments need not be long, but they do need to be informative.

> *Jason*
>
> *I'm facing the end of the first reporting period and the comments section of the progress reports. What should I include in the section requiring my comments?*

> The comments you make on the progress report can do one of several things. It can cause parents to call you for clarification, ask you for a conference, or clarify the grade or mark you have provided. Craft them carefully to be sure what you are saying supports the grade and expresses your intent.
>
> —Lisa, high school principal

Connect your comments to the learning goals, content, and skills students are learning:

- Refer to the notes you have made concerning students to help you recall important items to share.
- Prepare both generic and focused comments.
- Provide both positive and constructive comments.
- Be professional and avoid sarcasm or educational jargon.
- Be sure your comments reflect a true picture for parents. Review what you said.

If you are looking for a place to start, Google report card comments and you'll find many suggestions for your comments catalog. (→ See Resources and Online Appendix 10.1 for examples.)

Dealing With Political and Volatile Agendas

Sooner or later, you will find yourself encountering parents who may make things difficult for you. They may be angry with you concerning disciplinary actions or grades, or they may be angry with the school. They may also be angry and frustrated with what their child is doing (or not doing). Whatever their reason, they may become roadblocks to learning.

When a difficult situation arises, you must be prepared to stand your ground and defend actions taken. If you have kept records concerning student behaviors, they will be helpful in discussing the situation with parents as well as administrators. At the first sign of a confrontational situation, have a discussion with your mentor. Consider bringing in a colleague or your department chair, a guidance counselor, or the principal. Explain the situation and how you plan to proceed. Provide evidence and ask for input as to how this issue can be resolved. Be sure to review any school policies that may impact what you have done.

How do I handle a situation where the parent is very unhappy with a grade and challenges me?

Heather

There are many resources that can help you with defusing a situation and moving forward in a productive manner. Several strategies are important for you to learn:

- ☐ Disarm the criticism.
- ☐ Keep the conference discussion focused on your goals.
- ☐ Get a commitment from the parents to move beyond the concern and work together productively.
- ☐ If you are wrong, admit your mistake and apologize.

Most schools have a sign-in policy for visitors, including parents. But if a parent makes an unscheduled visit to your classroom when class is in session, follow the school's policy on this. For example, you could notify the office and ask the parent to return there until you are available.

In all cases, be a good listener and show empathy and concern. The parent must know that you are listening to their concerns.

Parents may show concern if they have a point of view that disagrees with what is being taught in your class. Be confident in what you are teaching. School policies concerning religious or political topics should be strictly followed. Be certain that you understand the school, district, and (in some cases) state requirements

> If parents are angry and blowing up at you, just be quiet and listen. They will not hear anything you have to say until they calm down. The best thing to say is, "I understand what you are saying." While they are venting, think of how you can work together to solve the issue and be prepared to tell them what you have done so far.
>
> —Sharon, grade 5 teacher

concerning topics such as dissection, sex education, evolution, use of the internet, and use of cell phones. Discuss with your mentor or administrator any possible controversial topics she has encountered. She will have a local perspective and be able to guide you through the controversies. Then deal with parent concerns by providing facts and regulations you have used.

If a parent becomes belligerent or hostile, you are not obligated to continue the conversation. Try to defuse the situation and do not argue or become hostile yourself. If necessary, thank the parent politely and professionally and end the call or conference. Document your conversation with as many details as possible. Then discuss the incident with your mentor or administrator.

Parent Resources

One of the best ways to create partnerships with parents is to engage them in your classroom as guest speakers or "experts for the day." Consider sending a questionnaire home to parents (or provide it during back-to-school night) asking for their background and what they might contribute to the class. You may want to list the general topics you will study this year and then ask questions such as these:

> Once you win parents' cooperation, everything else is a piece of cake.
>
> —Joclyn, grade 7 science teacher

- ❐ Do you have a hobby or vocation that ties to one or more of our science topics?
- ❐ Do you know experts in the scientific field who might visit our classroom?
- ❐ Do you or your employer have materials or equipment that can be shared with our students? (Determine the board of education's gift policy and be sure to check all equipment before you accept it. See Chapter 5 for more on lab equipment and supplies.)
- ❐ Would you be willing to serve as a chaperone for one of our field trips?
- ❐ Can the facility at which you are employed serve as a field trip site?
- ❐ Do you have a collection that can be shared in a display?

Take advantage of informal opportunities to interact with parents at school or community events.

Conclusion

Creating a partnership with parents will not only provide you with substantial support and resources but also result in increased student accomplishment and a positive attitude about school and learning.

Resources *(www.nsta.org/riseandshine)*

Report Card Comments

100 Useful Words and Phrases When Writing Report Card Comments for Elementary Students: *www.worksheetlibrary.com/teachingtips/usefulwordsforreportcards.*

html. If you are looking for modifiers and descriptors that will help express the accomplishments of students who are receiving specific grades (such as a C), this is a great site to help you craft your comments.

Comment Ideas for Report Cards: *http://teachnet.com/how-to/endofyear/ personalcomments061400.html.* You will find a collection of more than 300 general adjectives and phrases on this site.

How To: Report Card Comments: *http://teachersnetwork.org/ntol/howto/align/ reportsam.* Teachers Network has many resources for teachers. The report comments and phrases do not address science specifically but include speaking, writing, listening, general remarks, and phrases, as well as key terms.

Report Card Comments: *www.teach-nology.com/teachers/report_cards.* This is a members-only site that provides comments for all disciplines as well as behavior.

Report Cards: Advice and Suggested Comments: *www.teachervision.fen.com/school/ assessment/6964.html?&detoured=1.* This site provides comments and phrases in categories concerning work habits, personality and attitude, student behavior, academic achievement, and citizenship.

Report Designer: *www.bigwave.com.au/reports/bigsample.html.* This site contains comments indicating four levels of development for each category, including cooperation, following directions, independent worker, enthusiasm, work habits, use of time, and several disciplines of science. This extensive listing is a free sample. You may pay to access the entire site and develop your own list based on their large catalog.

Evolution

Evolution: *www.pbs.org/wgbh/evolution.* A resource from PBS, including videos for students and online courses for teachers

Evolution Resources: *www.nsta.org/publications/evolution.aspx.* A list of print and electronic resources compiled by NSTA, including a Q & A about teaching evolution

Evolution Resources from the National Academies: *http://nationalacademies.org/ evolution*

Intelligent Design on Trial: *www.pbs.org/wgbh/nova/evolution/intelligent-design-trial. html.* The website of the NOVA program documenting the court case of 2005.

Jensen, J. 2008. *NSTA toolkit for teaching evolution.* Arlington, VA: NSTA Press.

National Center for Science Education: *http://ncse.com.* Resources from an organization whose goal is to keep the study of evolution in public schools

National Science Teachers Association (NSTA). 2003. NSTA position statement: The teaching of evolution. NSTA. *www.nsta.org/about/positions/evolution.aspx*

Understanding Evolution: *http://evolution.berkeley.edu.* Tutorials and teaching resources, including a version in Spanish.

Dissection

National Science Teachers Association (NSTA). 2005. NSTA position statement: Responsible use of live animals and dissection in the science classroom. *www. nsta.org/about/positions/animals.aspx.*

Online Appendix

10.1 Progress Reports Comments Catalog

CHAPTER 11
FINDING SUPPORT

Dear Ms. Mentor,

What did you learn from your mentor?

Dear Heather,

I remember myself as a novice teacher years ago in a junior high school with some challenging students. I had a good background in the science content for the two subjects I was teaching, but I really struggled with classroom management. There were days I felt like I was on the *Titanic* with no room in the lifeboats. But my mentor must have recognized my potential. He observed some classes and threw me a lifeline.

His first suggestion was to establish routines for the beginning and end of class and transitions between activities. These are times when disruptions are likely to happen, so it is important for students to be engaged and know what is expected of them. He provided knowledge and experience and helped me organize lab materials for the two subjects I taught. Sometimes his assistance was in the form of a question: Why would you do a lab activity or give a test in both subjects on the same day? I learned that having routines and being organized provide time for more important topics and activities and can help prevent discipline or logistical issues.

He also asked another veteran teacher on the faculty to have lunch with me. I was in awe of her (she was a legend in the community) and hesitant to ask her for advice. She started our first conversation by inquiring about a group of students we had in common. When I described some of the challenges I was having, she said they tried to act the same way in her class. I felt like a weight was lifted off my shoulders—I wasn't the only one who had problems with these students! Together, we brainstormed some ideas to help these students stay focused and cooperative. I learned that I shouldn't take it personally when students misbehave.

My mentor also covered one of my classes occasionally so that I could observe other teachers. I noticed how one of them would stand at the door and greet the students by name when they entered the classroom. She also had a no-nonsense approach in terms of her expectations for acceptable behavior, but her classroom was a place where students were at ease and eager to participate. I had been told in a methods course that students need teachers who are fair, firm, and friendly. From this teacher, I learned what those characteristics looked like in a real classroom.

Some of the suggestions from my mentor and colleagues would have been second nature to a veteran teacher, but to a novice like me, they were life- (and career-) savers. When I had the chance to mentor new science teachers, I shared my experiences with them.

—Ms. Mentor

EVEN THOUGH YOU'RE surrounded by hundreds of people, teaching can be an isolating profession. It's important to realize that you are not alone. No matter how good your student teaching experience was or how well you know the content, when you have your own classes you'll find situations for which you are not fully prepared, and you can't solve every problem by yourself.

If you were successful as a student teacher, it can be a humbling experience to ask for or accept help and advice. New teachers are often embarrassed to ask questions or may feel they are intruding or being a burden. But everyone had to start somewhere.

Mentors

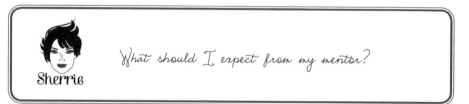

Sherrie

What should I expect from my mentor?

Schools often ask experienced teachers to serve as mentors for new teachers. Some schools have a full-time person to mentor several teachers; others use classroom teachers who agree to take on this responsibility in a one-to-one relationship with a new teacher. An effective mentor can be a role model, good listener, source of suggestions and resources, critical friend, or shoulder to cry on.

It's helpful if your mentor is another science teacher, but this is not always the case. If you and your mentor have the same planning period, it makes it easier to meet. But if you have different planning periods, it makes it easier to observe each other's classes. Your mentor may contact you before school starts, although some schools wait a few weeks before assigning mentors in order to determine the needs of the new teacher.

Mentors should be willing to share their expertise in a nonsupervisory relationship. A mentor is not judgmental or a "sage on the stage" who demands that you do things in a prescribed way. A good mentor should be a "guide on the side" who will offer advice and suggestions. A good mentor will encourage you to try new strategies and help you reflect on the results. Your mentor may even learn something from you as part of the process.

What should you expect your mentor to do?

- Meet with you at scheduled times—before school, after school, or during a common planning period. Later, these meetings could be on an as-needed basis.
- Assist you with understanding the curriculum, selecting instructional strategies, and designing assessments.
- Help you resolve issues related to classroom management and student behavior.
- Advise you on school policies and procedures (deadlines, paperwork, emergency plans).
- Share the school culture and alert you to some of the unwritten rules (so that you don't take someone's favorite parking space, for example).
- Introduce you to key people and help you form professional relationships.
- Be the go-to person to answer your questions—or help you find the answer.

Mentoring can be part of a formal induction program that is required in many schools as part of a strategic plan. Other parts of an induction program may include professional development opportunities for new teachers and observations by administrators. There may be required meetings, with forms to document the meeting times and events. If such a formal program exists in your school, you should receive a handbook or other documentation describing the components and requirements.

In an ideal situation, you and your mentor will form a close, supportive relationship. However, if your assigned mentor is not helpful or you're incompatible on a personal level, document your efforts to meet. After a few unsuccessful efforts, you can ask for a reassignment or look for informal mentors.

What should you do if your school does not assign a mentor? During the first week or so, try to get to know some of the other teachers. As you ask questions and talk with them, you'll probably discover a few helpful teachers who could serve as informal mentors.

Some teacher education programs at colleges and universities have follow-up activities for their graduates. These are often online communities in which you can connect with others in a virtual mentoring environment. Other online communities have been established by professional organizations (such as NSTA) to network new teachers with experienced ones. Listservs, blogs, and social media sites can be part of these informal networks. (→ See Online Appendix 11.1 or the resources in Chapter 9 for a list of professional organizations related to science education.)

> Our school has a luncheon for new teachers and their mentors before school starts and at the end of the year. This is a way to introduce teachers to each other, share stories, laugh at our mistakes, and celebrate our success.
>
> —Lisa, high school principal

Know Your Team and Department

 Who are the colleagues that can provide me with specific information?

Heather

At the beginning of the year, you met a lot of people. (→ See Chapter 2 for more about meeting the knowledgeable people at your school.) As the year progresses, advice from your colleagues can be helpful as a supplement to working with your mentor or within an established induction program.

Who are some of the key people who can help you?

- The science department chair can answer questions about ordering science equipment and materials: the timeline, how to prioritize your requests, and whether individual teachers submit requests or if requests are compiled by subject area. (Schools usually start preparing the next year's budget in January.) The department chair can also help you get additional supplies during the year. The department chair is often involved with curriculum design and textbook selection if you have questions.

- The school librarian (also called the media specialist or information technology specialist) can guide you to print and electronic resources related to your content area and offer suggestions for interdisciplinary connections and examples of projects that other teachers have done. If your students are working on projects, alert the librarian so that he or she can assist them.

- The teacher organization representative would be familiar with contractual issues such as pay and benefits, working conditions, or sick and personal days.

- The technology coordinator can assist with access to equipment that may not be housed in your room, maintenance issues, software updates, informal training, or instructional resources for you and your students.

- The guidance counselor can provide some insights into a student's background or recommend strategies to deal with students' needs.

- The special education supervisor can answer questions about students' individualized education plans. Many schools assign one special education staff member to students who are taught by the same teacher. That provides the staff member with continuity and an ability to serve the needs of the student and teacher. Determine if this is the case in your school and identify with whom you will be working.

- Stay on good terms with the support team (such as the office staff and custodians) with a friendly hello or compliment. An occasional thank-you note or holiday greeting is a nice touch (and your work may move to the head of the copier queue if you're in a rush).

> Unfortunately, some teachers are not very supportive of new teachers. They may be overwhelmed themselves, or they may think, "They should have learned that in college." These people may have a negative attitude and take out their frustrations on their colleagues (and perhaps the students). If you run into people like this, be polite but stay far, far away.
>
> —Ty, middle school principal

It may be helpful to form an informal support group with other new teachers. Even though you may teach different subjects, you'll find common issues in managing the classroom, dealing with students, and learning school policy.

You'll meet many of your colleagues at department, team, grade-level, and faculty meetings. As the "newbie" on the staff, you would be wise to begin by observing the personal dynamics and listening to the conversations. In these meetings, however, you don't have to be a silent observer. You can offer a fresh view of situations from the perspective of newer teachers. You may have skills in technology, writing, or presenting that may be useful. If you're a recent graduate, your science content knowledge may include experiences with cutting-edge topics.

You can also use your status as the new kid on the block to ask questions during the meetings: Why do we … ? What would happen if … ? What is the purpose of … ? If you get responses such as "We've always done things this way" or "We tried that years ago, and it didn't work," ask for clarification. These questions can lead to interesting discussions about school practices. Asking thoughtful questions can be just as much of a contribution as having the answers.

Greet other teachers (by name once you learn them) in the hallway or the lunchroom. Re-introduce yourself and ask questions. Everyone likes to feel needed, and you can gather advice from veteran teachers: "How do you handle tardy students?" "What do you do to engage students?" Even experienced teachers like to be recognized: "Your bulletin board gave me some good ideas." "My students were really excited about what you did in class yesterday." Listening to other teachers may reassure you that they have challenges similar to yours: curriculum pacing, classroom management, or district policies.

Surround yourself with colleagues who have a positive attitude and a sense of humor. If you're invited to join a group for a cup of coffee or dinner, accept the invitation. These social activities will help you learn the culture of the school. Positive colleagues can provide emotional support, model a can-do attitude, and share stories about their own early days to show that you are not alone.

Administrators

Some new teachers may be nervous about talking with administrators and asking for assistance. Will the principal think of these requests as a sign of poor preparation or incompetence? Try to develop a positive rapport with your supervisor so that you'll be comfortable asking questions or seeking advice. An approachable, supportive administrator is important for a new teacher, especially if you do not have or can't find a mentor from among the faculty.

Tanya

My principal stops by my classroom frequently. Does that mean that he thinks I'm not doing a good job?

Your principal may recognize the demands on your time as a new teacher and try not to overload you with extra duties (such as study halls or lunch duty) until you have adjusted to your new role. However, in some schools, it is the norm for new teachers to be assigned the most challenging classes and a full load of duties, "float" from one room to another, or teach in a room that is not set up as a lab. If you're in one of these situations, support from your mentor, other teachers, and the principal is important.

Some principals host lunch meetings or other informal gatherings to get to know new teachers and introduce them to other administrators. Take advantage of these or other opportunities to interact with the principal, assistant principal, instructional supervisors, and members of the office staff.

Your principal may observe you several times during the first year. This is often part of the district's professional development or induction plan. Many principals go beyond the basic requirements when working with new teachers. They may visit your classroom frequently to see how you're doing or share resources such as books, articles, or websites. This is not necessarily a sign that something is wrong. You may be using some interesting strategies that they would like to learn more about. You may be interacting with and reaching students that are a challenge for other teachers. Or you may have struggled at the beginning of the year and they're just checking in to see how you're progressing. A few words of encouragement or support from your principal can make your day.

There are issues that are beyond your control, and the advice or intervention from the principal is essential. Even experienced teachers need assistance with a violent student or an intrusive, demanding parent ($\rightarrow$ see Chapter 10, "Parents as Partners"). Your principal may want to sit in on meetings with parents, especially if the issue is a volatile one. When students are constantly disrupting your class despite your efforts to deal with the situation, ask the principal for assistance or recommendations. The other students will be grateful.

Invite the principal into your class to showcase areas in which you think you are doing an effective job. For example, if you have some strategies for using probeware or particular lab routines that work well, your principal may be interested in seeing your innovations. The ultimate compliment would be if the principal suggests that other teachers can learn from you!

> Some principals may seem aloof at first, but they may not want to interfere with your classes unless you ask for assistance or they see that things are out of control.
>
> —Lisa, high school principal

Conclusion

Even the most competent, professional teacher in the school was once a first-year teacher and faced issues similar to yours. Many of your colleagues will be sympathetic to your struggles and willing to help. Take advantage of their expertise and experiences. On a practical note, school administrators have a vested interest in your success. If you leave at the end of the year (or before), they'll have to go through the search, interview, hiring, and orientation processes again. Thus, they will want to do their part to help you succeed and remain at their school.

Resources *(www.nsta.org/riseandshine)*

Rhoton, J., and P. Bowers, eds. 2002. *Science teacher retention: Mentoring and renewal.* Arlington, VA: NSTA Press.

Zubrowski, B., V. Troen, and M. Pasquale. 2008. *Making science mentors: A 10-session guide for middle grades.* Arlington, VA: NSTA Press.

Online Appendix

11.1 Professional Organizations

CHAPTER 12
PREPARING FOR YOUR EVALUATION

> **Tanya**
>
> Dear Ms. Mentor,
>
> Our principal has started doing five-minute "walk-throughs" in our school. What can she learn from such a brief classroom visit? How should I prepare?

Dear Tanya,

While principals have always been out and about in their schools, "walk-throughs" or "learning walks" are becoming an accepted strategy to learn more about what happens inside the classrooms. Walk-throughs differ in format and purpose from the formal yearly or biannual observations in which the principal focuses on a single teacher for a longer period of time for evaluative purposes. Some schools refer to walk-throughs as visits to differentiate them from the more summative or contractual observations. Walk-throughs are not meant to be evaluative, and the feedback is usually not incorporated into the teacher's final evaluation.

These brief visits could be seen as checking the vital signs of a school. The principal gets an overview of what is happening in the classrooms across grade levels or subject areas, not just by walking in the hallways but also by stepping into classrooms on a frequent and regular basis.

Does your principal communicate what she is looking for in her visits? For example, if your school emphasizes strategies such as cooperative learning, writing in the content areas, classroom management, higher-order questioning, or technology integration, she may visit classrooms with these strategies in mind.

If your principal does not have a background in science education, you and your colleagues could help the principal understand what to look for in science classes: inquiry, safe lab practices, student engagement in teams, science notebooks, the use of technology, and authentic assessments.

You can compare walk-throughs and formal evaluations to your own behavior when students are working in small groups on projects or reports. As the teacher, you circulate around the classroom, briefly visiting each group, observing how they work together, checking their progress, answering questions, and providing encouragement and feedback. You probably do not grade these informal observations and interactions, but you do learn a lot about your students and what they are doing. When the students have finished their projects, you then formally evaluate the project with a rubric and give a score or grade.

You do not have to do anything special to prepare for these visits, nor should you change what you're doing when someone arrives. Continue your lesson while the principal is in the room. After the visit, you may get some feedback in writing. The principal may also stop by and talk with you about the visit, especially if he or she had questions or specific suggestions. If she does not provide feedback in a timely manner, ask her about what she saw and whether she had any questions or comments.

—Ms. Mentor

OUT OF THE corner of your eye, you see your classroom door opening. The students all turn around to see who's there. The principal tiptoes in and stands in the back of the room to observe your lesson. She may take notes. But don't panic. Take a deep breath, get the students' attention, and continue with the lesson.

Classroom observation, including walk-throughs, is a common component of supervision and evaluation systems. These systems are (or should be) designed to assess teacher quality and promote professional growth. In some schools, teacher evaluation is the principal's job; in others, the evaluation is conducted by other supervisors or peers. In addition to observations, your evaluation might include factors such as professional activities, progress toward personal goals, a teacher portfolio (including lesson plans and examples of student work), self-reflection, feedback from parents and students, and evidence of student learning.

Being Observed

> *Why is the principal taking so many notes during an observation? Does that mean I'm doing something wrong?*
>
> Jason

Being observed is a routine experience for veteran teachers, but for a new teacher it can be a stressful time. Your classroom may seem to have a revolving door, as you are visited frequently by an administrator (principal, assistant principal, superintendent, curriculum director, instructional supervisor) or another teacher (your mentor, the department chair, an instructional coach). In some school districts, the teacher contract specifies the purpose of formal observations and who is authorized to conduct them.

From a principal's perspective, visiting classrooms and observing teachers is part of his or her role as an instructional leader. Getting into the classrooms provides the principal with an up-close view of the teaching and learning that occur in the school. The visit provides another type of data to supplement test scores and attendance rates to get a complete picture of the school. Observations also give the principal a chance to see individual teachers in action, so he can identify teachers who are successful and those who are struggling. When visiting classrooms, the principal sees how students behave in various situations and how buildingwide initiatives and instructional programs are being implemented.

As a new teacher, you have a chance to demonstrate your abilities and show how you're improving. The students get to see the principal outside the office as an educator, not just the school manager or disciplinarian. Most of the time, they'll ignore the visitor, but they may appreciate the chance to show off what they're doing.

Don't panic if the observer takes notes during the visit. The district may have a form to follow for describing the class and providing feedback. These forms may have generic "look-fors" (teacher and student behaviors), but they could also focus on the components of initiatives or programs. The principal may have a paper version of the form, or there might be an electronic version on a laptop or handheld device. These notes will be helpful when the principal is back in her office and ready to share her thoughts with you.

After the visit, the principal will review her notes, and she should provide you with some feedback in a timely manner. She may give generic praise ("Good job!"), which is nice to hear, but it would also be helpful for her to note specific comments or recommendations, especially if they were identified look-fors. She may also ask questions to help you reflect on your strengths and needs. Depending on the type of visit and what was observed, the feedback may be provided in a written note, as an e-mail, or during a face-to-face meeting.

These visits can range from informal and impromptu walk-throughs to more formal, scheduled observations whose results become part of your yearly evaluation and are included in your personnel file.

> It's unfortunate that some principals view classroom visits as mere formalities. Some teachers may view them as unnecessary interruptions or distractions. But when they are done positively and professionally, the principal and the teacher (and the students) can benefit.
>
> —Lisa, high school principal

Walk-Throughs

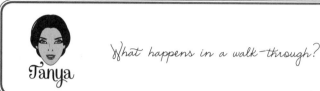

What happens in a walk-through?

Tanya

According to the Center for Comprehensive School Reform and Improvement (2007), a walk-through is a "brief, structured, nonevaluative classroom observation by the principal that is followed by a conversation between the principal and the teacher about what was observed." Protheroe (2009) describes characteristics of walk-throughs, including a focus on specifics, the critical role of feedback, and the value of reflection on the feedback. The literature usually describes principals as the observers, but walk-throughs can also be conducted by central office staff, instructional coaches, department chairs, project directors, teachers, or teams of teachers.

Walk-throughs provide candid snapshots of what happens in a class. A visitor can learn interesting facts about a class in just a few minutes. But these snapshots can also raise questions, especially about the context of the lesson and what preceded and would follow this brief visit. In a walk-through, the principal or other visitor enters the classroom unannounced at any time during the class period and stays for 5–10 minutes. He or she will watch the classroom events and probably take notes. The notes may include questions and anecdotal observations, or there may be a checklist of look-fors. (→ See Resources and Online Appendix 12.1 for examples of look-fors.) But remember that this is a brief visit. Don't think that you should have a check mark next to everything!

In some cases, walk-through data are collected, combined, and used by principals to determine a focus for the entire building or department. For example, if the science department has determined they should incorporate more inquiry, these walk-throughs can inform everyone if they are reaching their goal. (→ See Resources and Online Appendix 12.2 for information on classroom inquiry.) For that reason, walk-through observations are usually not included as part of the formal evaluation process and are sometimes referred to as "visits" rather than observations.

Some principals put time for walk-throughs in their weekly schedules. They view this time as an essential part of their day, and they visit each teacher several times each month. The key element of walk-throughs is not just checking off boxes on a form but also the reflective dialogue between the teacher and principal soon after the visit. These conversations can become opportunities to improve teaching and learning.

> At first, students were temporarily distracted when a visitor came in. But eventually, students saw walk-throughs as part of the school routine, not as interruptions. The students actually enjoy showing the principal what they're learning.
>
> —Shayna, special education teacher

Formal Observations

To expand the picture of what happens in a classroom, administrators also conduct formal observations of teachers during the year. These observations provide a different perspective from walk-throughs. These observations usually last for an entire class period, so the observer is in the classroom long enough to get a bigger picture of the teacher's classroom management skills; content knowledge; and ability to plan, conduct, and evaluate instruction in a cohesive and purposeful way. Formal observations are often used in a teacher's final evaluation. The teacher's contract may indicate that new teachers be formally observed more frequently than veteran teachers.

How should I prepare for a formal observation? What is the principal looking for?

Jason

Sometimes these observations are unannounced, but if the principal informs you of a date and time, you have the opportunity to plan, reflect, and get nervous! Some teachers suggest you shouldn't have to prepare anything—just teach what you ordinarily would. The reality for a novice teacher is that no day is ordinary. You are still developing your repertoire of effective teaching strategies. What your principal sees is a work in progress. There are some things you can do to help make this a positive experience.

Before the Observation

Talk to your mentor or another science teacher to find out what the usual procedure is for observations.

- Does the principal stay for the entire class period?
- Where does she sit? Does she walk around the classroom?
- Is there a particular form she uses to record her notes?
- Does she talk to the students?
- What kind of feedback should you expect?
- When do you get the feedback?
- Do you have an opportunity to discuss the feedback?

In some schools, the principal sets up a preobservation meeting, but even if that is not the case, you can still ask your principal ahead of time about her expectations. Does she want to see hands-on activities, large-group instruction, a lecture, the use of technology, a lab investigation, an assessment activity, classroom routines, or cooperative learning? However, you should not change the structure of your lessons to accommodate an observation. If the principal wants to see a particular activity, check your lesson plans and provide dates when you anticipate using the activity.

Take a quick look around the classroom or lab. It should be safe, organized, and conducive to learning. You don't need a new wardrobe, but your own appearance should be professional as always.

> Even the most carefully planned lesson can go awry. Ask your mentor or other teachers how they survived some of the events that may have happened during their observations: fire drills, street noise, interruptions on the PA system, power outages, or disruptive students.
>
> —Joclyn, grade 7 science teacher

> I ask all teachers to make an appointment with me to discuss their evaluations.
>
> —Ty, middle school principal

During the Observation

When your principal comes in, give her a copy of the lesson plan, along with handouts, the textbook, or other materials that will be used during the lesson, including safety goggles. If you have students with special needs in your class, provide that information to help the observer understand some of the accommodations you will make. Be sure you're using the required or suggested lesson plan format, rather than a list of assignments such as "Read Chapter 6" or "Lab on Fungi." If the lesson is a continuation from previous class periods, provide the principal with enough background on what the students did prior to this class, including the big idea or theme of the unit. Likewise, describe what the next lesson will include. As you begin the class, list on the board the learning goals for the day and the activities that will occur (this is a good teaching strategy even when you're not being observed.)

Since you have time to prepare for this observation, you could prepare your own list of "look-fors"—things you would like the principal to notice. If you have the opportunity, ask your observer to focus on one or two of these features:

- Your bell-ringers
- Class routines
- Use of science notebooks
- The way you pose questions
- Use of wait time
- How you and the students use technology
- Well-organized cooperative groups
- Lab safety procedures

Some teachers go overboard to create a show for an observation. A savvy principal will be able to tell whether she's seeing usual routines or contrived events. Some teachers inform the students about the observation ahead of time. The students may be nervous with a visitor in the room, although they should be familiar with your principal's presence from the walk-throughs and observations in their other classes. You may find that they'll be on their best behavior so that you get a good review.

If things go wrong or if there are interruptions, deal with them as you would if the principal were not in the room and continue with the lesson.

After the Observation

Ask the principal when you can meet to discuss the class, and use this time to share other information about the class. If the principal observed a lab class, describe what students learn from these activities (perhaps with examples of student work), the amount of time it takes to set up and put away the materials and read a report from each student, and the safety and cooperative learning procedures you use to help students learn.

Assuming she provides constructive feedback, with comments and recommendations, this could be an opportunity for you to grow as a teacher. Ask questions about how the lesson could be improved or about a strategy that wasn't working as well as you hoped. The principal may ask you questions such as these:

- Why did you choose this activity?
- Did the students learn what you wanted them to? How do you know?
- If you teach this lesson again, what would you do differently?

Don't think of these questions as criticisms; the principal may be trying to help you reflect on your decisions. After the meeting, save a copy of her notes or report and a summary of your responses.

It's normal to feel nervous, and even veteran teachers get a few butterflies when the principal walks in. Your principal is not expecting scripted perfection. She's more interested in your instructional strategies, how you convey your interest in the subject, how you relate to the students, and what your students are learning.

Reflection and Self-Evaluation

Reflection

At the end of each class or each day, record in a log or on your lesson plan what has occurred and where you need to go with the next lesson. Even if you teach several sections of the same course, each class has different needs, responds differently, and takes the instruction in different directions. This immediate reflection will help you with continuity and the development of subsequent lessons.

Give yourself a pat on the back for successes and think about how you can be even more successful. Give yourself permission to make mistakes and then learn from them. Note any questions or concerns. These few reflective minutes can also help you transition from the demands of the classroom to your after-school responsibilities.

Some teachers also like to arrive at school earlier than the required time. This quiet time allows them to prepare mentally for the day.

Self-Evaluation

In addition to an evaluation by a supervisor, you may want to do a self-evaluation. If you set professional goals at the beginning of the year, do a check at midterm and the end of the year. How did you do? What goals did you meet? What assistance do you need? If you were the principal, how would you rate yourself? On what evidence would you base your rating? If you're overwhelmed, choose one goal to deal with at a time. Start off with something that seems doable and check it off your list when it is accomplished.

As you look back over your journal notes, ask yourself how you have improved. How did you resolve some of the issues you faced at the beginning of the year? What were your "aha!" moments?

> Sometimes, we teachers are our own worst critics. We dwell on one little thing that went wrong in a lesson rather on than the things that went well. We berate ourselves for one inattentive student instead of considering the 24 who were participating and learning.
>
> —Dwayne, grade 9 science teacher

Is it a good idea to ask students for feedback on my teaching?

Alberto

Periodically asking students for feedback can be helpful in your self-evaluation. You can talk informally to individuals or small groups of students, create online surveys, or include questions on exit slips. Generic questions such as "What did you like?" may not provide as much useful feedback as focused questions such as "Which learning activity(ies) seemed to help you the most?" or "What can I do to help you?" You'll find that students can be brutally honest. (→ See Resources and Online Appendix 12.3 for student surveys.)

A very powerful method for self-evaluation is watching a video of one of your lessons. You can play the role of the principal as you observe one of your own classes, using the same criteria as the principal does. Some schools encourage teams of teachers to videotape each other's lessons and review them informally as a professional development activity. It's a humbling experience to see ourselves as others see us.

Final Evaluation

At the end of the year, you may receive a formal document with your final evaluation. Think of it as your own report card. This document differs from state to state, and your district may have additional documents beyond the required form. This compares to a summative evaluation, and you may receive a rating or points based on the criteria.

Check with your mentor or department chair to find out what this document looks like. Note the categories of criteria that are used in the evaluation. Some commonly used ones include planning and preparation, the classroom environment, quality of instruction, professionalism, student engagement, and/or content knowledge.

You should also find out whether other criteria such as test scores, grades, or student feedback are factored into your evaluation.

Documentation

My principal asked me for some "evidence" for a strategy I'm using. What can I provide?

Tanya

Your principal may ask you for some documentation as she completes your final evaluation. This documentation could include the following forms of evidence:

- Up-to-date lesson plans, using the designated template or your own
- Current student records (e.g., grade book or a summary of student grades)
- Records of professional development activities and meetings you attended
- Copies of communications to and from parents
- Discipline or incident reports that were filed and any follow-up you did
- Samples of student work (make a copy before you return it to the student)
- Samples of assessments and rubrics
- Photos of classroom activities
- Feedback from walk-throughs and observations
- Instructional materials that you created or adapted
- A log of time spent on science-related management: inventorying and maintaining the storage areas, repairing or servicing equipment, and complying with local and state safety regulations

Your first year is a good time to start a system for organizing your professional records and documentation into a portfolio. Keep your portfolio in a secure place. Back up any electronic documents and save them to a secure location.

Conclusion

Consider observations by others as opportunities to improve your skills as a teacher. Be proactive in providing your observer with as much information as possible to make their visit productive. Informed comments from an observer can help you identify your skills and grow as a professional.

Professional development and teacher evaluation are complementary processes. PD activities can help you improve your teaching skills, and feedback from evaluations (including observations and self-evaluation) can identify areas in which you could use additional PD.

Resources *(www.nsta.org/riseandshine)*

Examples of Look-Fors

Denver Public Schools: Best Practices and Look Fors in Science: *http://curriculum. dpsk12.org/math_science/science/best_practices/index.html*

Reformed Teaching Observation Protocol (RTOP): *http://physicsed.buffalostate. edu/AZTEC/RTOP/RTOP_full*

Science Classroom Observation Protocol: *http://cascadesolympic.mspnet.org/media/ data/Science_Classroom_Observation_Guide_REFERENCE_EDITION_4_1_. pdf?media_000000005767.pdf*

Technology Integration Matrix: *http://fcit.usf.edu/matrix/matrix.php*

Student Surveys

Aguilar, E. 2009. How to foster student feedback. Edutopia. *www.edutopia.org/ student-feedback*

Carondelet High School Science Teacher/Course Evaluation (Example of a student survey): *http://trampleasure.net/lee/wp-content/uploads/2010/08/Science-department-class-evaluation-Trampleasure-2010.doc*

Grading the Teacher: *http://fnoschese.wordpress.com/2010/08/11/grading-the-teacher*

Walk-Throughs

Protheroe, N. 2009. Using classroom walkthroughs to improve instruction. Principal (March/April). *www.naesp.org/resources/2/Principal/2009/M-A_p30.pdf*

Center for Comprehensive School Reform and Improvement (CCSRI). 2007. Using the classroom walk-through as an instructional leadership strategy. *AdLit.org. www.adlit.org/article/27501*

Online Appendixes

12.1 Examples of Look-Fors
12.2 Classroom Inquiry
12.3 Student Survey

CHAPTER 13
END-OF-YEAR ACTIVITIES AND REFLECTIONS

Sherrie

Dear Ms. Mentor,

I'm approaching the end of my first year as a science teacher. It was a challenge, but I learned a lot. Do you have any tips for what should I do or think about to prepare for next year?

Dear Sherrie,

Congratulations on completing your first year! You're probably counting down the days as students complete their final projects and assessments and as you enter their final grades. You'll also have inventories, reports, and other paperwork to complete. As you look forward to a break, it's tempting to wait until the next school year to clean up and organize your materials. But taking a little time now for these tasks will make coming back more pleasant and less stressful.

Your classroom may not be secure over the break, so that's another reason to inventory and secure equipment and materials *before* you leave. Take a look around the classroom or lab and storage areas. Did you store equipment and other items in an organized manner after cleaning them and making necessary repairs? Are the closets, cupboards, and drawers locked? Did you secure your personal items?

Packing up one year and preparing for the next involves more than physical resources. It's also important to pack up and prepare yourself professionally. While your memory is fresh, take some time to review and reflect on your experiences. To what extent did the students meet the learning goals of your course? Did you have to adapt or modify any of the goals? How well did you interact with the students? What did you learn about them? What did they learn about you?

Look back over your notes and reflect on the course curriculum and your lesson plans. Should you change the amount of time or emphasis you put on some topics? What did you do to guide students through inquiry and problem solving? How did you modify your instruction to meet students' needs? Were your lesson plans detailed enough to be adapted for next year, or will you have to recreate them?

What instructional strategies do you want to try next year? How effective were your classroom management strategies? Did your lab activities help students develop their inquiry skills? Were you able to access and use the technologies that are available in your school? What kinds of interdisciplinary connections were you able to make?

As you complete final grades for students, ask yourself how well the grades reflect students' achievement of the learning goals. Are you satisfied with your grading system? What opportunities did students have to reflect on their own learning?

Identify any gaps in your content knowledge that could be supplemented this summer with professional development opportunities or independent study. Based on your reflections, this might also be a good time to formulate your goals for next year. If you take some time now for thinking, reflecting, and planning, you'll have more time in the fall for getting your second year off to a good start.

—Ms. Mentor

ON THE FIRST day of school, did you ever think you would make it to the end of the school year? You're probably looking forward to vacation time with family or friends, graduate courses, home improvements, a summer job, or some much-needed rest. However, you'll find that the end of the year can be as hectic as the beginning, with exams, grades, inventories, and lab cleanup. Instead of saying, "I'll think about this later," spend some time getting reorganized and reflecting on your experiences now.

End-of-Year Learning Activities

Alberto

What kinds of activities could I use during the last few days to keep students interested and learning?

The last days of the school year can be just as challenging as the first. Students may believe that once exams or final assessments are over, the year is over too. Their attitude and behavior during these days can reflect this belief.

Perhaps this idea originated before the advent of electronic grade books, when teachers had to submit their grades a week or more before the last day of school so report cards could be finalized and printed. Students then assumed that activities during the last week of the term would not count. But with electronic record keeping, the results of learning activities can be documented up until the last day of school.

On these days, students may actually appreciate some purposeful activities, rather than free time, busy work, study halls, or long videos. You might consider these options:

- Games that actively involve students (or teams of students) and are related to course content or vocabulary, such as Pictionary, Jeopardy, or Password
- Student miniprojects, in which teams of students have a limited amount of time to prepare a skit, interview, video, or presentation on a course topic
- Time for students to make final entries or reflections in their science notebooks
- Online activities or simulations related to the course work or to preview the next course
- Lab investigations, one-class-period challenges, or brief lessons on topics you didn't get to during the year

Even though you received feedback from students during the year, the end of the year is a good time to capture their final perceptions. Some teachers use a structured teacher evaluation questionnaire, with questions that focus on their teaching strategies, availability, and communication skills, as well as the classroom climate (→ see Resources and Online Appendix 12.3 for student surveys). An open-ended survey can also get student views:

- What were your favorite activities (and why)?
- What topics were the most meaningful or interesting (and why)?
- How did the topics and the activities relate to your personal life or future goals?
- What is the most significant concept or attitude you learned in this class?

On the last day, put on your warmest smile and say good-bye to the students. Tell them you'll miss them and you look forward to seeing them next year, even if

> Students need to participate in learning activities up to and including the last day. Don't pack up your stuff or take down bulletin boards before the last day, if you can help it. Students get the message that the year is over if the room is bare and they are no longer engaged in classroom work.
>
> —Lisa, high school principal

they won't be in your class. But remember that not all of your students are looking forward to lazy days, summer camp, and family vacations. For many students, school is a safe haven, with caring adults, warm meals, and interesting things to do. They will miss school, even if they don't want to admit it!

The Year in Review

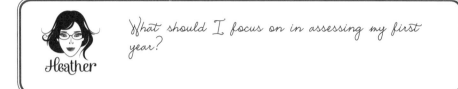

What should I focus on in assessing my first year?

Heather

After the last class leaves, your classroom will be unusually quiet. But before you start your own activities, take some time to reflect on the year in terms of student learning, the curriculum, and lesson planning. Be honest with yourself. Learn from your challenges and celebrate your successes. Review your journal notes and record your final reflections.

In some schools, there is scheduled time at the end of the year for new teachers and their mentors to meet. Some principals also schedule meetings with new teachers to debrief on the year's accomplishments.

Student Learning

As you look over your gradebook or class rosters, think about the students who made your classroom a lively and interesting place:

> I like to come back to school the day after the last day of school. It's usually very quiet and I have time to reflect while the memories are still fresh in my mind.
>
> —Pat, grade 11 science teacher

- Which students seemed to improve academically through the year? What did you do to encourage this improvement?
- Did some students seem to regress during the year? How could you tell? What could you do if this happens again?
- What strategies did you use to connect with students and encourage their participation? Were they successful? Are there any new strategies you would like to try next year?
- How effective were your classroom management routines and rules? Should you make any changes?
- Did your students seem to enjoy learning? How do you know?
- What about your students surprised you the most this year?
- How did you encourage parental support and engagement?

As you complete final evaluations and grades for students, ask yourself these questions:

- How well do the grades reflect actual student learning rather than student behavior or other factors not related to the learning goals?

- How well did your assessments align with the unit goals and lesson objectives?
- Did you provide opportunities for students to reflect on their own learning (e.g., through a science notebook, rubrics, or self-assessment)?
- What kind of opportunities did students have to demonstrate their learning? What choices did you provide (e.g., projects, tests, demonstrations)?

Curriculum and Lesson Planning

Consider your course curriculum and the instructional resources that were available to you:

- Did some lessons have different results than you anticipated? What did you learn from these experiences?
- Should you change the sequence of topics or the amount of time or emphasis you put on them?
- Did you use an effective combination of science content, skills, and processes?
- Did your students have the prerequisite skills or knowledge you expected? If not, how could you adapt your instruction to help them meet the learning goals of the course?
- How were you able to access and use the technologies available in your school? Do you need additional training or practice?

Although some schools do not require you to write detailed lesson plans, there are advantages to having plans that can be revisited and adapted the following year:

- Were your lesson plans detailed enough to be adapted for next year, or will you have to recreate them?
- Based on your formative assessment data, what instructional strategies should you add, change, eliminate, or keep?
- How were your in-class and homework activities aligned to the unit goals and lesson objectives?
- Did your lab activities help students develop and use their inquiry skills? How do you know?
- How did you adapt your instruction for students with disabilities?
- How did you adapt your instruction for English-language learners?
- What kinds of interdisciplinary connections did you make?
- What technology applications did you incorporate into your lessons?

Look back at your philosophy of education that you composed at the beginning of the year ($\rightarrow$ see Chapter 1 for more on your teaching philosophy). How did your experiences this year correlate to this philosophy? Should you make any changes to it? Your reflections and feedback from your mentor and principal will also be helpful in preparing for next year.

Inventories

 Tanya *What will I have to do before I leave my classroom on the last day? May I leave personal belongings at school?*

There are practical considerations at the end of the year too. Ask your principal, department chair, mentor, or the building secretary about any end-of-year checkout procedures. Find out when (or if) you will have access to your classroom or lab over the break, the hours the building will be open, and if you must turn in your keys.

As a science teacher, you are responsible for several inventories. Take care of these before you lock the door for the break. Keep in mind that your classroom may not be secure during maintenance or renovation activities.

Classroom or Lab

- You may be required to hand in a room inventory with the number and kinds of desks, chairs, and other classroom furnishings.
- Update the science equipment inventories, including any equipment that you added, discarded, or gave to another teacher.
- Note if any equipment needs to be repaired. Find out from your department chair how to get these repairs accomplished in a timely manner.
- Put all lab equipment and materials in locking cabinets or secure storage rooms.
- Make sure items such as glassware, cages, aquariums, sinks, or tabletops are clean and ready for next year.
- Turn off the gas and water in accordance with school policy.
- Return any materials you borrowed from the library or other teachers.
- Find a home for classroom animals and plants (→ see Chapter 5, "Safety in the Laboratory").
- Take photographs of your classroom or lab before you leave to document what is in place.

Textbooks and Technology

- Inventory the textbooks so you'll know if you have enough when you get your new class list.
- Ask the librarian for advice on repairing damaged books. If any are unusable, ask about your school's discard and replacement procedures.
- Follow your school's requirements for inventorying and securing technology such as laptops, desktop computers, projectors, speakers, calculators, handheld devices, and cameras. Although some schools allow teachers to take their assigned computer and other technology home for the summer, don't take any school equipment out of the building without permission.
- Notify the technology coordinator of anything that should be repaired, replaced, or upgraded.

> Before the textbooks are turned in, I have my students clean out any papers or sticky notes, erase any marks, and let me know of anything that requires my attention, such as graffiti, torn or missing pages, or water damage.
>
> —Sharon, grade 5 teacher

- Find out if you will have access to your school e-mail over the break so that you can keep up with your correspondence.

Personal Items

- Take valuable belongings or irreplaceable mementos home or lock them in a cabinet.
- Label your personal items and keep a list of what you leave in the classroom (items can "disappear" over the break).
- If you have to turn in your laptop or desktop computer, transfer personal documents, tests, grades, or other sensitive information to a secure network drive or a flash drive. (Check with an administrator for any regulations on how long you must keep student grades or other records.)

Teachers are notorious pack rats. If your course documents are saved digitally, it's not necessary to save multiple paper copies. Recycle any extra handouts or use the blank side for scratch paper or quizzes.

Some of your equipment (e.g., balances, laptops, electronic probes, calculators, projectors) may have value outside of school and could be targeted by thieves. Be sure serial numbers are inventoried and equipment is labeled with the school name (your maintenance staff may have tags or standardized ways of labeling). Keep these items locked up, and if you notice something is missing, report it immediately to the principal.

Professional Activities

> *After taking care of inventories and grades, I'm now beginning to think about what I need to do to grow personally in preparation for next year. I'll begin by going back through this book, but what else should I think about right now?*
>
> **Jason**

As a professional, you have responsibilities for continuing education and maintaining your credentials. Set up a file in which you can save appropriate documentation for these activities (→ see Chapter 12 for more on documentation). Take some time over the break to accomplish the following tasks:

- Expand your own content knowledge with graduate classes, online courses, readings, websites, or visits to informal science institutions (museums, zoos, parks, planetariums, etc.).
- Improve your teaching skills (instructional strategies, assessment, technology, classroom management) through webinars, online courses, readings from professional publications, study groups, or social media sites.
- Update your professional vita, noting the title and dates of workshops, conferences, or other professional development activities in which you

> I thought that because I'm "just" a teacher, I wouldn't have much to put in my vita. But when I start to write everything down, I discover that I accomplish a lot each year.
>
> —Dwayne, grade 9 science teacher

participated. Include extracurricular activities you supervised, volunteer work (such as tutoring, judging a science fair, or planning a field trip), memberships in professional organizations, and committees on which you served (→ see Resources and Online Appendix 13.1 for examples).

- Create a folder for the year to save copies of any certificates or records of attendance you received at workshops. Also, save recognitions you may have received or positive notes from parents or students.
- Send a brief note of thanks to those teachers and other staff members who were particularly helpful to you this year.
- Revise your goals for next year (→ see Online Appendix 13.2 for a goal-planning guide).

Conclusion

Spend a little time at the end of the year organizing your materials and reflecting on your experiences. When you do finally close the door, you'll be ready for the challenges at the beginning of the next year. And don't forget to spend a little time on yourself over the break.

Resources *(www.nsta.org/riseandshine)*

Student Surveys

Aguilar, E. 2009. How to foster student feedback. Edutopia. *www.edutopia.org/ student-feedback.*

Carondelet High School Science Teacher/Course Evaluation (Example of a student survey): *http://trampleasure.net/lee/wp-content/uploads/2010/08/Science-department-class-evaluation-Trampleasure-2010.doc*

Grading the Teacher: *http://fnoschese.wordpress.com/2010/08/11/grading-the-teacher*

Résumés and Vita

Elementary School Teacher Sample Résumé: *www.resumepower.com/Elementary_ School_Teacher_Resume_Sample.htm*

Résumés for Teachers: *www.money-zine.com/Career-Development/Resume-Writing/ Resumes-for-Teachers*

Writing the Curriculum Vitae: *http://owl.english.purdue.edu/owl/resource/641/01.*

Online Appendixes

13.1 What to Include in Your Professional Vita
13.2 SMART Goals

EPILOGUE

YOU ARE A valuable asset to your school. Don't underestimate your abilities and the influence you as a teacher can have on students. Make that influence a positive experience. Most of your students will not go on to become professional scientists, but with your guidance, they'll see the importance of science in their daily lives as parents, taxpayers, informed citizens, and voters. Think of all the amateur astronomers, rock hounds, bird-watchers, naturalists, gardeners, and inventors who were inspired by their science teachers to engage in science-related hobbies and avocations.

Successful teaching is both a skill and an art. All of the techniques you learned in college did not by themselves make you a competent teacher. Like any other skill, competence comes with experience and practice. The art of teaching also evolves from experience. No college course can tell you how to determine which technique is most effective for a particular student, how to adapt inquiry lessons to match the experiences of *your* students, how to handle the recalcitrant student or unhappy parent, and how to vary the content to engage the different students in each class. Every year you will learn more as you add ideas or teaching strategies to your repertoire. Every year, your experiences and reflections will make you a better teacher.

As you reflect on the year, consider what you have provided to students. Some students (and parents) make great sacrifices to attend school. They may be responsible for taking care of younger siblings before and after school. Some take public transportation or walk long distances to attend school or find a quiet place to study after school. Others give up paying jobs to be in school. Consider the learning opportunities you have provided—have they been valuable and worth the sacrifices for them to be in your class each day?

We asked our new teachers: What were your big "aha" moments during the year? What will you do differently next year? Did you get any advice that was especially helpful?

- I learned that with younger students, you have to be alert. They are fun to work with, but it was a challenge to find ways to take advantage of their enthusiasm. Establishing routines was a big help. If they did act out, I learned not to take it personally.
- The best advice I received was to do a lot of modeling. We assume that students know more than they really do. Once I modeled how to take notes, for example, the students caught on quickly.

- I devised an organization system using color-coding, labels, and storage boxes, and I didn't leave a disorganized classroom behind at the end of the day, even if I had to stay a little longer.
- I was advised to start a portfolio with copies of exemplary student work. I'm going to share it with my students as samples and models of the highest quality work and to see how student work has changed over time based on how I've have adjusted the lessons.

- I learned not to take myself too seriously! I made a lot of mistakes, and it helped to laugh along with the students. Lab safety, however, was not a laughing matter. The contracts that I had my students sign showed them that I meant business.
- My mentor suggested that I start a file to keep positive notes from parents and students. I added notes about funny things that happened in the classroom and student success stories. I would revisit the file when I felt down.

- Don't sweat the small stuff (and most stuff is small). After establishing some basic routines and rules, I could relax with my students. I found I didn't need lots of elaborate rewards and incentives to keep students engaged, as long as I could help students see how the topic we were learning had real-world applications.
- My mentor suggested some online PD opportunities that were very helpful and convenient. I'll continue them next year, and maybe I'll even have ideas to contribute.

- My "aha" was learning to care for myself. I made time in my schedule for exercise and my fossil-collecting hobby, and I packed a lunch each day with healthful foods as an alternative to the cafeteria.
- I was advised that if I wanted to incorporate more inquiry into my science lessons, I should do this one lab at a time and not try to rewrite everything that has been done in the past all at once. I now have quite a few revised lessons, and I'll do more next year.

Think about science teaching and the joy that you get from being with students. Let your students feel that every day. No one is perfect, and even those teachers you admire as the best have had difficulties at some time in their career (probably at the beginning). Don't look at the teacher you are today and think you will always be this teacher. You will grow and learn. With your eyes wide open, this will happen every day because every day is different in a classroom.

We wish you the best in this career—one that can be filled with joy, excitement, and new experiences each and every day.

Our best wishes,
Linda and Mary

REFERENCES

Association for Supervision and Curriculum Development (ASCD). 2008. What students want from teachers. *Educational Leadership* 66 (3): 48–51. *www.ascd.org/publications/educational-leadership/nov08/vol66/num03/What-Students-Want-from-Teachers.aspx*

Brienza, V. 2011. 10 most stressful jobs of 2011. CareerCast. *www.careercast.com/jobs-rated/10-most-stressful-jobs-2011*

Brookhart, S. 2008. *How to give effective feedback to your students*. Alexandria, VA: Association for Supervision and Curriculum Development.

Bybee, R. 2006. *The BSCS 5E instructional model: Origins, effectiveness, and application*. Colorado Springs: BSCS. *www.bscs.org/bscs-5e-instructional-model*

Carlson, A. 2009. What students expect from teachers. Teachers at Risk. *www.teachersatrisk.com/2009/09/06/what-students-expect-from-teachers*

Center for Comprehensive School Reform and Improvement (CCSRI). 2007. Using the classroom walk-through as an instructional leadership strategy. *www.adlit.org/article/27501*

Children's Defense Fund. 2011. Core beliefs and educational philosophy. *www.childrensdefense.org/programs-campaigns/freedom-schools/about/core-beliefs-philosophy.html*

Colker, L. J. 2010. 12 characteristics of effective early childhood teachers. *Beyond the Journal*. Washington, DC: NAEYC. *www.naeyc.org/files/yc/file/200803/BTJ_Colker.pdf*

Curwin, R. L., A. N. Mendler, and B. D. Mendler. 2008. *Discipline with dignity*. 3rd ed. Alexandria, VA: Association for Supervision and Curriculum Development.

D'Arcy, J., and P. S. Della Rocco. 2001. *Air traffic control specialist decision making and strategic planning—A field survey.* Washington, DC: U.S. Department of Transportation. *http://dodreports.com/pdf/ada389823.pdf*

Durham Public Schools. 2008. Core beliefs and commitments. *www.dpsnc.net/about-dps/board-of-education/core-beliefs-and-commitments*

Fredericks, A. D. 2005. Too many tasks, not enough day. TeacherVision. *www.teachervision.fen.com/classroom-management/new-teacher/48351.html*

Gardner, H. 1999. *Intelligence reframed: Multiple intelligences for the 21st century.* New York: Basic Books.

Goodenow, C. 1992. School motivation, engagement, and sense of belonging among urban adolescents. Paper presented at the annual meeting of the American Educational Research Association, San Francisco. *http://eric.ed.gov/ERICWebPortal/search/detailmini.jsp?_nfpb=true&_&ERICExtSearch_SearchValue_0=ED349364&ERICExtSearch_SearchType_0=no&accno=ED349364*

Haskvitz, A. 2002. Top 11 traits of a good teacher. Reach Every Child. *www.reacheverychild.com/feature/traits.html*

Hunter, M. C. 1994. *Enhancing education.* New York: Prentice Hall.

Johnson, D. J., R. T. Johnson, and E. Johnson Holubec. 1991. *Cooperative learning in the classroom.* Edina, MN: Interaction Book Company.

Keeley, P., F. Eberle, and L. Farrin. 2005. *Uncovering student ideas in science, vol. 1: 25 formative assessment probes.* Arlington, VA: NSTA Press.

Marzano, R. J. 2007. *Art and science of teaching.* Alexandria, VA: Association for Supervision and Curriculum Design.

Marzano, R. J., D. Pickering, and T. Heflebower. 2010. *The highly engaged classroom.* Bloomington, IN: Solution Tree Press.

McLeod, J., J. Fisher, and G. Hoover. 2003. *The key elements of classroom management.* Alexandria, VA: Association for Supervision and Curriculum Development.

Miami Museum of Science. 2001. Forms of alternative assessment. *www.miamisci.org/ph/lpdefine.html#AA*

Mueller, J. 2010. Authentic assessment toolbox. *http://jfmueller.faculty.noctrl.edu/toolbox*

National Research Council (NRC). 2011. *A framework for K–12 science education: Practices, crosscutting concepts, and core ideas.* Washington, DC: National Academies Press.

National Science Teachers Association (NSTA). 2004. NSTA position statement: Scientific inquiry. *www.nsta.org/about/positions/inquiry.aspx*

National Science Teachers Association (NSTA). 2007. NSTA position statement: Liability of science educators for laboratory safety. *www.nsta.org/about/positions/liability.aspx*

New Leaders for New Schools. 2011. Our core beliefs. *www.nlns.org/CoreBeliefs.jsp*

Protheroe, N. 2009. Using classroom walkthroughs to improve instruction. *Principal* 88 (4): 30–34. *www.naesp.org/resources/2/Principal/2009/M-A_p30.pdf*

Raynaud, M. n.d. What do students expect from their teachers? QualityTime-ESL. *www.qualitytime-esl.com/spip.php?article317*

Redmond School District. 2007. Core beliefs, values, & commitments. *www.redmond.k12.or.us/14541013164911523/lib/14541013164911523/Core_Values.pdf*

Rivers, J. 2010. 12 of the most stressful jobs in America. Billshrink. *www.billshrink. com/blog/8642/12-of-the-most-stressful-jobs-in-america*

Rothstein-Fisch, C., and E. Trumbull. 2008. *Managing diverse classrooms.* Alexandria, VA: Association for Supervision and Curriculum Development.

Smyth, E. 2011. What students want: Characteristics of effective teachers from the students' perspective. Faculty Focus. *www.facultyfocus.com/articles/philosophy-of-teaching/what-students-want-characteristics-of-effective-teachers-from-the-students-perspective*

Texley, J., T. Kwan, and J. Summers. 2004. *Investigating safely: A guide for high school teachers.* Arlington, VA: NSTA Press.

Tolison, B. 2008. Top 10 most stressful jobs. WCTV. *www.wctv.tv/news/headlines/17373899.html*

Tomlinson, C. A. 1999. *The differentiated classroom: Responding to the needs of all learners.* Reston, VA: Association for Supervision and Curriculum Development.

Tracey, M. D. 2010. Top 10 most stressful jobs. *International Business Times.* U.S. edition. *www.ibtimes.com/contents/20100930/top-10-most-stressful-jobs.htm*

Wasserman, L. 2010. Teaching secrets: What kids wish teachers knew. TLN Teacher Leaders Network. *www.edweek.org/tm/articles/2008/09/17/02tln_wasserman.h20.html*

Wiggins, G., and J. McTighe. 2005. *Understanding by design.* 2nd ed. Alexandria, VA: Association for Supervision and Curriculum Design.

Wilms, J. D. 2000. Student engagement at school: A sense of belonging and participation. Organisation for Economic Cooperation and Development (OECD). *www.oecd.org/dataoecd/42/35/33689437.pdf*

ABOUT THE AUTHORS

Linda Froschauer began her 37-year teaching career as an elementary school teacher and went on to become a middle school science teacher, science department chair, and adjunct professor. Outside the classroom, she has worked as an instructor for Chicago's Museum of Science and Industry; as a writer and consultant for many publications; and as a field editor, reviewer, and consultant for numerous organizations. Since leaving the classroom, Froschauer has served as the editor of *Science and Children*, the National Science Teachers Association's (NSTA) journal dedicated to the improvement of science instruction in grades preK–6.

For nearly 40 years, Froschauer has been a leader and active member of NSTA and many state and national education organizations. During her involvement, she has served on many boards, including AAAS Project 2061, NSF Panels, Rosalind Franklin Society, and standards and frameworks committees. She has held many leadership positions, including the presidencies of NSTA, the Council for Elementary Science International, and the National Middle Level Science Teachers' Association. Her dedication to science education and classroom excellence has been recognized through several awards and recognitions, such as the Presidential Award for Excellence in Mathematics and Science Teaching, recognition by Southern Connecticut State University as Alumnae of the Year, and selection as an AAAS Fellow. Other awards and accomplishments include receiving the NSTA Middle Level Distinguished Teaching Award, the Educational Press Association of America's Distinguished Achievement Award, National Board for Professional Teaching Standards certification, the Connecticut Science Supervisors Association's Charles Simone Award for Outstanding Leadership in Science Education, selection as a Connecticut Science Educators Fellow, and being named Weston Teacher of the Year.

Froschauer earned a BS in education from Northern Illinois University, an MA in science teaching from Governors State University, and a sixth-year degree in curriculum and supervision from Southern Connecticut State University.

Mary Laverty Bigelow cannot remember when she was not interested in science. With support from her family and teachers, she has expanded that interest into a lifelong career in science education. As a secondary science teacher for 27 years, she helped students explore their world and provided many hours of professional development and support for other teachers. She spent an additional 7 years as a specialist at a regional service agency in projects related to professional development, classroom observations, data analysis, evaluation, and technology applications, with a focus on math-science partnership programs and reading and writing in the content areas.

She has taught graduate-level courses for teachers (both on-site and online) and has presented more than 50 sessions at state and national conferences. She was also the cofounder and editor of a journal related to teacher leadership and action research. She was the recipient of an Outstanding Teacher award from the Shippensburg University School Study Council and recognized as Teacher of the Year by her school district.

Since her retirement in 2007, Bigelow has been working on several projects for NSTA, including writing the *Ms. Mentor* and *SciLinks* blogs. She is also a consultant for NSTA websites and publications and for other agencies and organizations related to education. She is an avid bird-watcher, an amateur photographer, and a volunteer for local environmental projects.

Bigelow earned a BS in secondary education (chemistry), an MEd in academic curriculum and instruction (science education), and a PhD in instructional systems, all from The Pennsylvania State University.

INDEX